"*I believe it would startle and move anyone if they could make a certain effort of imagination and read it (The Bible) as a Book. . .*"

Robert Louis Stevenson

The *Distilled* Bible

The essence of the Bible

Not a revision
Not a translation
Not a paraphrase
Not an expansion
Not a Bible Story book

Instant comprehension
Can be read in 3 hours

A simple retelling
The best preparation
for the new Bible student

LIST OF AUTHORITIES
(representative)

The Holy Bible: King James Version

George Ricker Berry: THE INTERLINEAR GREEK—
ENGLISH NEW TESTAMENT

F. F. Bruce: THE EPISTLE TO THE HEBREWS

Coneybeare and Howson: THE LIFE AND EPISTLES
OF ST. PAUL

Alfred Edersheim: THE LIFE AND TIMES OF JESUS
THE MESSIAH

Charles Hodge: ROMANS; I, II CORINTHIANS

H. A. Ironside: REVELATION

Robert Leighton: COMMENTARY, I PETER

Lockman Foundation: THE AMPLIFIED BIBLE

John R. Rice: PRAYER: ASKING AND RECEIVING

H.D.M. Spence; Joseph S. Excell: THE PULPIT
COMMENTARY

James Stalker: THE LIFE OF JESUS CHRIST

Spiros Zodhiates: THE BEHAVIOR OF BELIEF (JAMES)

The *Distilled* Bible

New Testament

Roy Greenhill

Paul Benjamin Publishers
Stone Mountain, Georgia

The *Distilled* Bible / New Testament

Paul Benjamin Publishing Co.
P.O. Box 1207
Stone Mountain, Georgia 30086

Library of Congress Catalog Card Number: 79-56356
ISBN: 0-936950-00-5

Copyright © 1980 by Roy Greenhill

Cover Design: Don Rogers
House Editor: Daniel Streib
Layout Artist: Julie Olson Breedlove
Mass Market Distributor: Henry Freeman

Printed in the United States of America

CONTENTS

To believe,
to have confidence in tomorrow,
to know there is love
from God
for you and others.
That is the evident purpose
of the Holy Bible.

"And Philip ran thither to him, and heard him read the prophet Isaiah, and said, Understandest thou what thou readest? And he said, How can I, except some man should guide me?"

Acts 8:30-31a

Matthew

In a totally surprising manner, the hopes of mankind are about to be fulfilled. That great Leader who is to be crowned by God, King, Prophet, and Priest, and who has been long and ardently desired by man the world over (especially the people of Israel whose Book and history are the source of the hope) is to appear. But how different He will be from all men's dreams!

THE PREPARATION AND THE PREACHING

Israel knew exactly from which ancestors their Messiah would arise, and they carefully kept the family records.

Jesus of Nazareth met those ancestral requirements as well as the prophecy that He would be born of a virgin.

Learned men from distant lands knew it was time for His birth, and some came bringing birth gifts; but the king of His own land sought to murder the infant Christ.

With the financial help of the foreign visitors, the humble parents took their Holy Treasure to hide in Egypt while the maddened king slaughtered babies without mercy.

Then, in Nazareth, a village in northern Palestine, He spent His childhood.

In the year 27 A.D., a thundering prophet was speaking to great crowds, announcing the Day of Hope. Many were eager to be prepared, but this John 'the Baptist' culled out the hypocrites and promised them the anger of the Messiah.

When he saw Him, he knew in an instant that this Jesus was to be the Anointed One. And Jesus knew beyond all doubt that He himself was the Messiah.

Once divinely empowered for His mission, Jesus was tempted to take unethical short-cuts, but He chose to work strictly according to the Hebrew Scriptures.

Then, after John was imprisoned for his courage, the Nazarene began His ministry—in His home district of Galilee. He called four fishermen to be leaders of men. His work brought Him immediate fame and huge crowds from the entire Roman province of Syria.

Jesus so hated the idea of being a hypocrite that He continually spoke to those who had received the born-again life John and He had been preaching, telling them exactly how to live:

THE SERMON ON THE MOUNT

'The Kingdom of Heaven' is *the Presence and Blessings of God.*

With the key of sincere faith, open the door of happiness, and no problem can close it.

Only happy believers can help humanity and lift the lost.

Only a humble heart can understand the Bible.

Murder is bad, but so is disrespect for any man. God hates both and will not overlook either.

Simply make a habit of telling the truth and you will not have to punctuate your speech with oaths.

Only fake love leaves out enemies. God loves His enemies. His love is perfect.

To please God one must secretly give his charities, and offer private, simple prayers. But even the best of prayers,
You are my Father
I want Your blessings
I ask Your help
I need Your mercy
Be Thou my Guide
— is empty words without sincerity.

9

Show-off religion is insincere.

You will not please God if you worry about material things. Worry will destroy your Heavenly treasures, turn your knowledge into ignorance and make you a slave to 'things.'

Worry insults God. God will take care of you—forever.

The way to improve others is to pay attention to your own imperfections—not theirs! Forcing improvement upon others will only cause them to hate you.

Success is answered prayer.

If you can't get your prayers answered, you surely can't live the Golden Rule.

False doctrines are simply eruptions of evil hearts. Every heart will be exposed at the Judgment.

Humble faith will pass the Judgment but insincerity will bring eternal disaster.

THE MIRACLES AND THE MESSENGERS

Jesus did many miracles:

He healed a leper—but not as a device to excite the masses;

He healed a Roman soldier's servant—betokening the evangelizing of the nations;

He healed Peter the fisherman's mother-in-law—so she could serve her Saviour;

He filled a night with healings at the synagogue in Capernaum—just for pity;

He calmed the sea—in the crossing of Galilee the boat would not wait for those looking for greatness, and would not sink with those who loved Jesus;

He healed the minds of two wild men—but was expelled by hostile Gentiles;

He healed a paralyzed man at Capernaum—after He forgave his sins;

He saved a cynic—Matthew, the crooked publican; (Jesus had come for the guilty who were ready to admit it. The Old Day was of God, but the New Day offered these greater things.)

He cured a bleeding woman—while moving through Capernaum on an errand of mercy—her faith stood out in the crowd;

He raised a little girl from death—just as a mother sweetly awakens her children;

He healed two blind men—although there was danger of unwanted publicity;

He gave speech to a voiceless man—and was cursed by the leaders.

Jesus loved the abused, the ignorant and the poor. And He had a plan to help:

11

Jesus' CHARGE TO THE MINISTRY:

You Apostles are to minister to the two million of Galilee, with any helpers you can enlist. Offer God's presence to the Jews, and find the most receptive. Expect official opposition—even some loved ones will oppose—but death itself can not interrupt your peace in the presence of God.

I will also join in the campaign.

Preach the whole story with deep awareness of the eternal punishment of the lost, and of the constant care of the Father for His children.

You, and all soulwinners, will be rewarded in Heaven. (Those who oppose the Gospel will be destroyed forever.)

The soulwinner may be disowned by his family. But every individual must keep his own conscience—and bear the cost. The soulwinner and his helpers have found the closest possible relationship with God!

THE PROGRAM AND THE PARABLES

John the Baptist was reassured and praised by Jesus, because, the New Testament, which would bring far greater blessings than the Old, had been inaugurated with total success.

He should have been accepted as the forerunner of the New Day. But, most leaders did not want any style of truth. Those with the greatest spiritual opportunity had neglected it. Their political hopes were empty!

Only the utterly sincere could comprehend why God offered spiritual help, when everyone thought the problems were political. But this spiritual help lifted the burdens of the *heart* and gave eternal peace to the *soul*.

A day of rest was given in mercy. But Israel's leaders did not understand that the Sabbath was given to help mankind; therefore acts of mercy and necessity were always legal.

Jesus is the Lord of Mercy!

He demonstrated this by healing a man's deformed hand—and the Pharisees displayed their Sabbath devotion by plotting to kill their Messiah.

Jesus withdrew into the crowd and cautioned against stirring emotions in the street that could be interpreted as political organizings.

When the Saviour healed a voiceless blind man, the people were astounded—but the Pharisees cursed Him.

Jesus answered their illogic by declaring His ministry to be the Kingdom of Heaven warring against Satan's kingdom, and He pressed the point by identifying Satan's soldiers!

Although you may misunderstand what you SEE, when you choose the wrong side in the INVISIBLE war you have chosen eternal loss.

It is the time to get the unseen right!

The Pharisees' hearts were exposed by their words. They still wished to see something, but Jesus promised them punishment because they had opportunity, and abused it.

The born-again have new hearts, giving them kinship with God.

Jesus taught PARABLES BY THE SEA. (Parables, because people only hear what they are prepared to hear; sincere listeners understand while hypocrites continue in confusion.) Jesus' students were getting to the *inside* of life.

THE SOWER: Comprehension is essential to learning. The ability to comprehend depends upon the preparation of the individual. Sincerity is the essential preparation!

THE WHEAT AND THE TARES: My mission is to the entire world. And no one, however sincere, has the ability to judge who is saved or lost.

THE MUSTARD SEED: The born-again can be assured of the magnificent power of a worldwide spiritual ministry.

THE LEAVEN: In the spiritual realm, truth

and freedom grow, and grow—and grow!

(These powerful concepts are new to humanity. The Gospel alone determines eternity, and Jesus alone will know who is lost and who is saved.)

THE HIDDEN TREASURE: *The spiritual life is priceless joy for all people.*

THE PEARL OF GREAT PRICE: *All who know what the heart longs for will choose the Gospel at any cost.*

THE NET IN THE SEA: *The decision demanded in the Gospel is the most pressing matter of time and eternity.*

THE SAVIOUR AND THE SERVANTS

Decisions were made about the Saviour.

In the town of His childhood, Jesus was scorned and remembered as just a village boy.

Herod the Tetrarch heard of Jesus' fame and thought He was John the Baptist, whom he had killed to honor a lust-induced vow.

When Jesus sought privacy to contemplate John's death, He was followed by thousands— and they had to eat. A little food became much when He multiplied it.

Then Jesus again sought solitude on a mountain, and from there saw storm-tossed disciples. At 3:00 A.M. He walked on the sea to rescue

15

them, (Peter could have done it!) and blessings were brought to the other side.

The teachers and leaders of Jerusalem came to Capernaum to denounce Jesus, but He exposed their sin of greed as He publicly condemned them.

Peter did not understand the point that one cannot *eat* sin—so Jesus spoke bluntly:

> *Sin comes from the 'heart'—not the stomach.*

Then Jesus sought quietness in Phoenicia; but a determined woman needed help. Even though she was before her time, Jesus granted to her her every desire.

Returning to Galilee, Jesus met large crowds in Decapolis. These excited Gentiles needed food also. So, the Saviour organized and fed them all.

Then He sailed up the west coast of the lake.

When an unlikely coalition of Jews sought to bait Jesus at Magdala, He sailed on to the northern shore and warned the disciples concerning the rapid growth of false ideas.

In Caesarea Philippi, the disciples confessed the deity of Jesus—the cornerstone of the New Church.

Then Jesus, the Son of God, Israel's Messiah, turned to the Cross—which is our example, for it speaks of salvation and the beginning of the New Church.

On a mountain in Galilee, Jesus' deity was displayed to apostles of the New Church and to Moses and Elijah from the Old.

Jesus was steeled for His coming ordeal by the Father's voice. The Old has passed away! (This would be understood only after the resurrection.)

John the Baptist would have brought the Old graciously into the New, but the power of bigotry prevailed!

Below the mountain, Jesus healed an insane boy and explained the power of belief in the Holy Spirit and the use of prayer and fasting.

The pace to the Cross quickened.

There were many considerations in the new program of God. The children of the True Temple should not have to pay taxes to the old; but not to comply with custom would injure many people.

The Saviour taught His servants, ON GREATNESS:

> In the spiritual realm, the meek and lowly are the highest officials. And those who refuse to give spiritual tribute to them will be punished by the Great King. They are constantly remembered in Heaven, and their salvation is celebrated.

17

Congregations of born-again people must be organized around the forgiveness of one another and the presence of the Holy Spirit.

How much forgiveness? Those who have received eternal forgiveness must FOREVER forgive anyone as many times as he asks!

And the forgiveness must be sincere.

THE REJECTION AND THE REPLY

Jesus ministered in Judea and taught.

Gentleness and kindness will cement any marriage; but selfish sin destroys the union.

Many marriages are bad because many people marry who are not fully qualified.

Jesus endorsed child evangelism for the New Church.

Young adults may be interested—and very receptive to religion; but when Christ calls, the lust for wealth may be so great with those who seek it that they are almost beyond hope.

The quest for spiritual wealth may be costly—only God knows how much for some. God will reward according to His knowledge, and many will be surprised in

18

*That Day, who will never have guessed
the sacrifices some have made.*

Jesus led the way in sacrifice as He moved
toward the Cross.

James and John should have understood that
the necessary cost of great reward may be the
forsaking of life. The great spiritual leader is the
one who sacrifices for all.

Even in great excitement, Jesus was moved
by suffering, and healed two blind men.

Jesus entered Jerusalem as the prophet
Zechariah had foretold. Huge crowds cheered
the way, arresting the city's attention. He again
cleansed the Temple (as He had done exactly
four years earlier), healed the suffering, and was
recognized as Friend by a children's choir.

To pass the night, He returned to Bethany.

In the morning the Messiah cursed a fig
tree—barren like God's Temple. This was done
through the power of prayer.

The Temple authorities disliked His assump-
tion of authority, but could not answer His
wisdom.

*I lift the dregs of humanity above the
rulers who rule God's vineyard in the
tradition of murderers, and who are now
ready to kill God's Son.*

*You will lose the presence of God and
be destroyed! Your rejection of*

19

opportunity—with ridicule—will bring judgment!

Now all nations are to be invited—with acceptance demanded on a strictly personal basis!

The Pharisees sought an infraction of Roman edict; but money and taxes were not Messiah's issues at all. Then the Sadducees questioned doctrine, but Jesus contrasted ignorance with knowledge.

The Pharisees did not know that the Law has only one point, LOVE. They also missed the truth about the deity of the Messiah.

Jesus preached against the Temple authorities, O JERUSALEM, JERUSALEM :

Their legitimate authority is to be honored, but all are to ignore their examples: oppressing mankind, displaying religion, and lording over people.

Mankind must be loved and served; but these professional religionists are harassing humanity. They cannot see the spiritual world, they cannot read the Law, they have nothing for the heart, they cannot recognize death, they imitate their worst heritage.

THEY WILL SPEND ETERNITY IN HELL AND BRING DESTRUCTION TO THEIR NATION— WHICH COULD HAVE ENJOYED THE GOSPEL AGE!

THE DEPARTURE AND THE RETURN

Jesus preached to His disciples, THE DESOLATE TEMPLE AND THE PLAN OF GOD:

The Temple shall be destroyed and an Age closed. Confusion will be easy over these points; but remember that the world will continue in turmoil, and true disciples will have to endure persecutions, suffer desertions, face fanatics, and live with little love.

But they shall stand in the Judgment!

The Gospel will reach the whole world before the destruction of the Temple. The suffering then will be unspeakable, and absolutely devastating to the Old Order.

After the loss of the Temple, deceivers will set dates to confuse the New Church. No dates or signs will be necessary, for, after the final turmoil, the Second Coming itself will be the sign of the Last Harvest.

The destruction of the Temple is certain, and can be seen approaching, because it is quite near. The dissolving of sky and earth is sure also, but cannot be seen coming.

As the Great Flood came without any signs, so, before the Judgment there will be a 'Rapture'—without any signs.

21

This is the pertinent thing in prophecy for all born-again believers. It is the 'Blessed Hope,' the neglect of which will bring sorrow and loss.

THE BRIDESMAIDS: *The 'Rapture' will be a blessing only for the born-again. Those who reject reality and therefore do not prepare to meet God will miss the 'Rapture.'*

THE MONEY TRUST: *The churches are to multiply all blessings received.*

Unlike businessmen who increase their investor's money, Christians have a tendency to forsake soulwinning. People, in whatever field of work, who enhance their trust are honored. But unaggressive orthodoxy has forgotten this fundamental truth.

A New Church is replacing the Old Dispensation, paralleling the fundamental principle of economics.

The world's gain is Israel's great loss.

I will judge all peoples. No one will be able to claim the blessings of God if he has neglected the downtrodden, the bruised, and the brokenhearted—with whom I have eternally identified.

My anger against this callous oversight is undiluted by any circumstances. NOTHING CAN BE SAID!

THE CRUCIFIXION AND THE COMMISSION

The Cross was at hand, and Jesus dated His death.

The rulers plotted His death.

When the disciples saw extravagant love, they made a logical error, for they did not understand how close was the end.

An apostle joined the intrigue. Jesus ate the Passover feast with His Apostles, knowing that one of them was disloyal. He accused Judas.

The Saviour instituted the communion service, which is a picture of His Passover blood creating the New Church and an anticipation of the consummation of the eternal purpose.

Jesus felt very, very alone as He faced His ordeal of humiliation and disgrace!

As He prayed in the Garden with all human anguish,—not desiring death—Peter, James and John did not sense the test of rushing events.

Jesus, the Man, surrendered to the Father's plan of redemption.

It was the severest of human anguish—*dignity disgraced.*

Jesus was ready.

Ready to suffer a friend's betrayal. Ready to do the will of the Father. Ready to expose the cowardice of His enemies. Ready to endure the

23

weakness of His followers—who had neglected fortifying prayer.

Jesus was ready for His trials.

The masterminds awaited with wicked cunning; but lying hypocrisy was unanswered.

The High Priest asked the real question, and the reply was fearless truth—eliciting the sign of blasphemy, and uncovering the depth of human sin.

In the hour of trial, a base denial disgraced an apostle.

Jesus was taken before the governor.

(When the traitor saw his guilt and executed himself, the Temple rulers finally did something for the poor.)

He answered Pilate, but ignored the chief priests. Pilate had a plan to thwart their envy. (And God had spoken to his wife.) But the Temple rulers swayed the crowds who then gave the cry of infamy, shocking even a heathen despot— who chose an impossible position.

Jesus was humiliated, and delivered to death amid ignorant scorn. And, though He was weak, He suffered without flinching.

The Saviour was executed with thieves, and was mocked by passers-by, by Temple rulers, by dying sinners.

Ignorance and oppression seemed to win.

The Old was finished.

Death was conquered—to the wonder of witnesses.

Jesus was crucified, dead, and buried.

The authorities, gripped by anxiety, unwittingly guaranteed the credibility of the resurrection report—they guarded the corpse.

Jesus arose after the Sabbath passed and appeared to many! Disciples ran with the good news.

Enemies of the truth could only lie.

Before His ascension, Jesus, in a farewell address, gave the GREAT COMMISSION to the New Church:

Go, and present a New Day of love, of hope, of faith to the whole world!

Mark

The good news of the person and work of Christ was introduced to the world by John the Baptist. Although John himself was a striking personality, he was completely absorbed with this greater Person—who was one with the triune God, yet a man like all other men.

Jesus continued John's ministry of preaching the new birth and of enlisting disciples. He taught with authority and healed with power, immediately producing widespread consternation. His healings were both private and public, but not for publicity. He was a tireless worker, and found His power in the practice of prayer.

He preached and ministered throughout Galilee. His healing of a leper was to be told to the spiritual leaders, but not to the public, so as to protect the volatile populace from political arousal. Yet, excitement over Jesus was so great that crowds thronged Him in every city He entered.

In the meeting-house at Capernaum, as crowds packed the doorways, one man, in desperation, found a way to Jesus through the roof. He found Jesus, salvation, and health (in that order). The religionists were amazed at the miracle of healing but shocked at Jesus' forgiving the man's sins.

All religious leaders should preach forgiveness of sins. Healing is but a minor token of the power of the Holy Spirit.

The Saviour called a hated publican, sought out his 'sinner' friends, and identified them as the object of His mission.

Jesus differed from John; Jesus brought a New Day and a New Church.

He differed, too, from the legalistic religious leaders. And He addressed their wickedness.

Almighty God never intended His laws to be a burden upon life. All of His works are done for love of mankind. Failure to see this basic principle reveals a heart of stone.

The loving, powerful ministry of the Lord Jesus drew great crowds of common people (but only plots of destruction from their leaders). He was forced to retreat, by land and sea, from the throngs. Apostles were named to assist His ministry.

His family feared He was being carried away by the excitement, and His enemies suggested that He worked for a demon underworld.

If love is evil, there is no evil. No, God and Satan are both real, and those who confuse the two will inhabit Hell.

Jesus ignored His family's fears and turned to His family of the born-again.

Vast crowds listened as Jesus taught them in parables. Those who wanted to, understood, while hypocrites continued in their confusion.

He taught of a planter's problems—birds, stones, drought, weeds; and of his productivity. For some who asked, He carefully explained the meaning.

The planter is the soulwinner. His problems are Satan's false teachers, hearts of selfish pride and greed—unwatered by sincerity—and materialism.

The productivity of good ground varies according to the individual's understanding. God desires truth to be understood; but comprehension will not be forced, any more than financial success is forced.

When a person chooses to understand spiritual things, the Holy Spirit begins to work by taking the first small comprehension and multiplying it into enormous blessings.

Hypocrites will not believe this. How can they, being too insincere to receive the first small seed? They have cursed God's power.

29

Once, when Jesus and His friends crossed the Sea of Galilee, His peace in the face of a raging tempest illustrated for them that true spiritual understanding will result in moment by moment trust.

But the disciples counted themselves unworthy of the power of such peace.

In Gadara, a raging man recognized Jesus as his only hope. The demons deeply afflicted him, but Jesus transferred them into pigs. The power of Jesus to heal this troubled mind caused the poor, ignorant Gentiles to fear, and they begged Jesus to leave. Since they were not looking for a revolutionary hero, Jesus urged the delivered man to give a full report.

It was different in Jewish territory. There, an Elder of the people worshipped Jesus, begging Him to come to his dying daughter. (En route, Jesus honored the mere touch of faith from a woman seeking His healing.) The Elder's little girl had died, but *faith* was alive. When Jesus, with His apostles, reached the home, the skeptical crowd was expelled, faith surrounded the girl, and she awoke to a call of endearment. Here, secrecy was again enjoined, for the real danger of political application was great among the Jews.

The Saviour of the World was scorned in the village where His family still lived. That the heart of Nazareth was so hard saddened Jesus.

The great interest of other towns required His sending of evangelists. They took with them only His authority—not money (visible or hidden), nor tokens of wealth. They depended on God's friends.

Jesus' fame brought His name to the king, who thought He was John the Baptist, whom he had murdered for his condemning of adultery.

This Herod had been impressed with John, but flaming passion had overwhelmed him, costing John's head and the king's soul.

Amid great excitement the evangelists completed their tour. They began a retreat with Jesus, only to be interrupted by a demanding throng.

Jesus cared for all their needs; so, after detailed organization, He miraculously multiplied fish and bread.

Jesus then sent the apostles to Bethsaida by boat. Viewing them from a mountain, He walked across the stormy Sea to calm their distress. But, they still did not learn the lesson of peace in a troubled world.

Disembarking, they again drew huge crowds, to whom Jesus ministered, as always.

Jerusalem rulers found Jesus and questioned Him of their rituals (which related to their belief that evil resides in material things). Jesus attacked their foolishness, for they were filled with greed, and had lightly cast aside their holy duty.

> *Sin is not within matter, but in man's spirit. The heart is the womb and reservoir of sin. It disgorges filth which degrades human dignity.*

Jesus continued His search for a retreat, but in Phoenicia a desperate Gentile woman would not be denied. Later, on the long return trip around the eastern shore of Galilee, Jesus healed a deaf and speechless man. The fame of Jesus could not be hidden, for His power was so perfect.

Great crowds of Gentiles lingered in Decapolis, and they had to be fed (as earlier did the Jews). Jesus took His disciple's bread and multiplied it for thousands.

Back in Galilee, Jesus was annoyed by sign-seekers. He warned them of ignorance and wicked attitudes which His followers must learn to reject.

In Bethsaida, a blind man was healed, not with ritual, but with the anointing spittle of Jesus—simply because the Saviour loved him.

In an area of pagan towns, Jesus' Jewish disciples privately confessed Him to be Messiah. Again, however, public enthusiasms could not be trusted.

Jesus knew He had to die and rise again.

Peter would not hear it! Jesus explained the *spiritual* burden as opposed to *political* and *material* hopes.

The new birth of the individual must be fearlessly preached.

Then, the Messiah promised His apostles a vision of the coming blessing, and it was granted when the 'Law' and the 'Prophets' joined Jesus in the Transfiguration.

At this point, Peter felt he had to say something. But only the Father knew the grand significance—the deity of the Son. It was too much to understand at that moment, but everything was readying for the final events before humanity's New Day.

Down from the mountain, Jesus found a mute boy who was demonized. Any man of faith could have healed the boy. Jesus asked for the father's faith, and it was honestly and haltingly stated. Jesus expelled the demon—He was a man of prayer and fasting.

After a year's absence, Jesus had re-entered Galilee to begin His march to the cross. His disciples were dreaming of greatness, so Jesus explained His concept of leadership.

The weak must be served by those who would be leaders, and all who serve mankind in the name of Jesus must be honored. Those who oppose the powerless and poor, whose only hope is

33

in God, will burn in Hell. (The fires of Hell preserve while they punish, so, the punishment is eternal.)

As salt preserves the dead animals awaiting burning on the Altar, likewise God's leaders must be salted for death— living sacrifices. If they seek prominence, they stink with the unsalted rot of ambition.

As Jesus approached Judea, He was asked about divorce.

A selfish heart produces divorce, for it does not permit itself to be glued to another and fused with another. Selfish divorce, whether by men, as Jewish law permits, or by women, as Roman law allows, is adultery.

Jesus was loved by the little children.

Materialism grows with age.

A young man was interested in salvation, and he tried to be moral, but above Jesus' love he preferred wealth—and sadness.

For a rich man to be saved is rare, though not impossible.

Soul-winners who have left all have gained all—eternally. But only God knows who has really sacrificed.

Jesus was to soon sacrifice all.

Two apostles still thought of prominence, ignorant of its cost—death destiny.

Everyone must realize that I am against dictators and hierarchies. My concept of leadership is breathtakingly new. I will follow it through at the ultimate cost.

As Jesus entered Jericho, a well-known blind beggar begged for help. Jesus was moved, and healed the man's sightlessness.

As King of Peace, the Messiah rode the symbol of a triumphant ruler into Jerusalem. He surveyed the Temple and retired to a nearby village.

Returning the next day, He cursed a 'hypocritical' fig tree, and then cleansed the fruitless Temple of the crooks of Annas (the senior High Priest)—striking fear and astonishment.

From the example of the withered fig tree Jesus taught the lesson that power in prayer comes from a pure heart.

On the third day, in the Temple, the authorities questioned Jesus' authority, but could not answer His wisdom. He spoke to them of their responsibility as Israel's guardians.

You will be held accountable for the deaths of the prophets—and now of God's Son.

You have lost everything.

On the fourth day, men who were ordinarily mutual enemies combined against Jesus, to trap Him in political positions (He was totally non-political) or in theological debates. He stood on the Old Testament Scriptures, which guarantee a resurrection.

A sincere teacher of the religious Law began to see the truth (which all scribes should have known) that Messiah is deity. (But they were concerned only with show and greed.)

A poor widow stood above those of showy wealth.

Jesus predicted the end of the whole system, and the apostles asked for indicating signs.

There will be no sign. The born-again will be persecuted as they preach the Gospel. Their comfort will be the Holy Spirit. Hatred will test true love. Now, the destruction of the Temple will have a sign (of despair), but after its destruction there will be no signs of any kind until the second coming of Christ. The Temple's destruction can be anticipated, but the end of all things cannot. Believers must be alert 'day and night.'

As the rulers plotted to kill Jesus, He was anointed with love.

I have championed the poor, but fleeting opportunities to show love must be grasped when one can.

*And love will do what it can—as this
woman's deed will ever tell.*

Jesus had arranged a Passover supper. At the
meal He predicted betrayal. Here, He also instituted the Communion service, picturing His
substitutionary atonement.

Jesus was to be forsaken by His friends, even
Peter.

The Saviour prayed in Gethsemane.

He did not wish to die, but it was the Father's
plan.

The apostles could not grasp the drama.

The Temple police shattered the silence of
the Garden.

A kiss was placed.

Friends who were slow to understand were
quick to flee.

Mark, a teen-ager, was the last to leave.

Jesus was arraigned before some of the
Sanhedrin. False accusers were brought, but He
would not answer their perjuries.

He confessed His Godhood.

Caiaphas signaled 'blasphemy!'

The prisoner was mauled by Jewish guards.

Peter denied. And wept.

Soon after daybreak the entire Sanhedrin
sent Jesus to the Roman governor.

Jesus answered Pilate, but only stared at the chief priests.

Pilate would have released this victim of envy, but the priests stirred the mob which had assembled at the governor's balcony.

So a murderer was discharged instead.

The Roman soldiers mocked and beat the Son of God.

A Roman passer-by bore Jesus' cross to the execution site.

The Sufferer refused an opiate.

They crucified the King of the Jews—with criminals.

The passing throng gave jeers.

Chief priests and convicts mocked.

Jesus suffered in darkness. Alone.

Jesus' death brought a new dispensation of access to God—pictured in a Roman soldier's faith, and the devotion of womanhood.

A devout and prominent man received the body after Pilate confirmed death.

Two Marys planned corpse preparations.

Mankind's New Day began on the first Lord's Day.

—With an open tomb.

—With an empty grave.

—Amid excitement and confusion, and with appearances of the risen Christ.

The New Day brought a Great Commission, which will succeed whenever Christians go forth.

Luke

The good news of Jesus has been told and retold many times. Now everyone needs a carefully researched authoritative edition, covering all subjects from a universal perspective.

Zechariah, one of twelve thousand Jewish priests had long prayed for a son. An angel announced the answer and also provided proof—by suspending the old priest's ability to speak.

Elisabeth, so long childless, rejoiced in her honor.

A young virgin, Mary of Nazareth, was also promised a Son—THE MESSIAH OF MANKIND, whose conception in her womb would be a miracle. (Elisabeth's son was to be answered prayer

Mary visited Judea, ninety miles away. The beauty of Mary's unborn Son inspired exultant joy in Elisabeth and the virgin responded with her 'Magnificat.' After the three month visit, Elisabeth delivered John. His birth aroused local interest, and father Zechariah pronounced a benediction.

Augustus Caesar, the Emperor of Rome, registered his subjects at their birthplaces. Since empires do not wait for peasant babies to arrive, Mary's Son was born out-of-doors, where the poor live close to the ground. There, God hallowed a temple for angel choirs.

Humble shepherds were the first to spread the glad tidings.

Baby Jesus was immediately identified as a true son of Israel and THE SON who would fulfill her destiny. Jerusalem, the Holy City of David, bore witness through aged Simeon's song and prophecy. And Anna, so old and pious, spoke for the Temple of God as she reported the dawn of redemption.

In preparation for manhood, the lad Jesus returned, at age twelve, to the Temple, to ask and listen—and decide. His unusual understanding impressed His mother and it grew throughout the years of His preparation.

John, in his early thirties, was burning with God's message and he began preaching that each individual Jew must have a new heart to enjoy the New Day which was arriving immediately. He promised judgment for insincere religious professionals.

Born-again proof was demanded of all— from the Jews—from the 'sinners'—from the pagan Romans!

John the Baptist could easily have claimed

Messiahship, but he promised Another, who, he said, would immerse the born-again in peace and flaming love, and send the insincere to Hell.

Herod the Great's son, the District Governor of Galilee under Tiberius Caesar at Rome, imprisoned John—some weeks after the great preacher baptized Jesus, initiating the Saviour's ministry.

Jesus, also in His thirties, met the Jewish age requirement for Priesthood, and His ancestry met the prophetic qualifications to be the Priest of all mankind: it was traced from Mary, and her father Heli, through King David to Abraham, to Seth, to Adam, and to God. And Jesus was a man among men, tempted—to misuse His powers—to misplace His ambitions—to adopt meaningless methods to achieve His purposes. He resisted all.

Jesus' ministry brought Him immediate fame and success. At His boyhood church, He made an official presentation.

I am the Priest of the Poor: I mend broken hearts, I liberate troubled minds, I bring the lamp of true knowledge, I declare war on all tyrants. Humanity's day is here.

I don't expect acclaim in My home town, for like Elijah and Elisha, My greatest work will be among the strangers of the world.

43

The congregation's shock turned to rage. They wanted to throw Him over a cliff and drop boulders on Him.

The Saviour moved to Capernaum, twelve miles away, where He addressed great crowds and healed many disturbed minds. Everyone was taken with amazement. Here He lived in Peter's home. He healed the apostle's mother-in-law, and many, many others.

The Saviour's first grand tour began shortly after He preached from Peter's boat and directed a great catch of fish. He enlisted the four fishermen disciples to be full-time soul-winners.

Because He wanted Israel's leaders to know of His miracles (He avoided publicizing them generally), Jesus opened the tour in Capernaum at a convention of religious teachers. When a paralyzed man was lowered through the synagogue ceiling, the Saviour pronounced forgiveness of his sins. This infuriated the teachers. Their anger, though, was muted when Jesus immediately ordered the forgiven paralytic to stand up and carry his stretcher home.

Jesus saw many instant conversions, such as Levi, an extortionist tax-collector. This convert wanted his sin-sick friends to know Jesus.

I am always ready to house-call on 'sinners.' My followers do not fast (now) for they are celebrating a new thing which, in no wise, can fit into the old systems of religion. There is a New Day coming.

As the second year of Jesus' ministry opened, Sabbath-keeping had become a major issue.

A Roman officer who honored Israel was helped by Jewish synagogue officials. They begged Jesus to heal the man's dying slave. Then, other friends of the Gentile brought his plea. Jesus, greatly impressed by the soldier's earnest faith, healed his servant instantly.

Then Jesus traveled twenty-five miles from Capernaum to Nain, to a funeral of a widow's son. For pity of this woman, He raised her son. The effect was electrifying throughout the land.

When John the Baptist heard of Jesus' mighty works he wondered why the Messiah wasn't taking stronger national action. Jesus promised John's messengers nothing but continued acts of divine-human compassion. His respect for the forerunner was great.

He is a pillar of strength, living a life of sacrificial dedication. More than a preacher, he performs an historic service in the ushering in of God's New Day.

John's ministry had been essential to Jesus' own success and they had the same enemies.

You religious bosses cannot be pleased by any sincere person. John was a 'loner' and I am a 'mixer,' and you slander us both. Wise people do not judge by arbitrary personal styles.

Once while Jesus ate with Pharisees, a prostitute interrupted the meal and poured perfume on His feet. The unwise host was offended, but Jesus instructed him in the wisdom of a forgiven sinner's gratitude.

Forgiveness produces love, and that love cannot find enough to do to express the gratitude of the forgiven soul. I have forgiven this woman's sins. She is born again — there is nothing against her.

So, with the twelve, Jesus toured Galilee, financed by well-to-do born-again women. He taught His helpers to understand people.

People have varying capacities to assimilate truth. (Some have chosen to have no capacity at all to understand life.) There are those, so dominated by group pressures, that they can hardly hear God's message; others are greatly hampered by their backgrounds, and still others are so undisciplined in every respect that they cannot follow through with the knowledge they theoretically accept.

Truth appeals to noble instincts and underlying character. And then, truth MUST be shared — it is incompatible with secrecy. Failure to share knowledge insures its loss.

Jesus could not bow to His family's lack of comprehension.

Spiritual affinity is greater than natural relationships.

Once in a stormy crossing of Galilee Lake, He prayed the waters down. Then, on the Gentile side, He was met by a deranged outcast. The demonized man was calmed by Jesus. The destructive forces within him were as great as those which tossed the unruly sea.

The citizens were more afraid, in their ignorance, of the Saviour's power than of the wild man, so they turned Jesus away. The born-again man was left as an evangelist.

Back in Galilee, the choking crowds included a synagogue officer whose one and only daughter was dying, and a woman with a chronic hemmorrage. The woman touched the Healer, but the little twelve year old girl died. The home was filled with mourners and mockers. After expelling them, Jesus awoke the child. But He wanted no publicity.

Jesus formally commissioned His Twelve Apostles to do His very same works.

You need no physical provisions. Count as heathen those who refuse to help you.

Herod Antipas heard that Jesus was actually John the Baptist (whom he had killed) who had

47

arisen from the dead to work miracles. When the Apostles returned from their evangelistic tour, they and Jesus sought a retreat near a remote fishing village.

But thousands followed the preachers. Jesus taught them, and when it was time to eat, He divided up the crowd and miraculously multiplied a little food. (This was symbolic of how He would have spiritually fed all Israel.)

The apostles had heard all the opinions about Jesus, but they confessed Him to be the Messiah.

Keep this quiet, for there is a great drama of passion and resurrection yet to occur.

I am not to lead a war against Rome; in fact, My followers must simply prepare to be martyred, and then live each day as if their last. This is My prescription for victory. Political victories are hollow for men who do not know this personal triumph and the daily presence of God. Those who ignore this will be greatly embarrassed in the Day of Triumph. Some of you will see this victorious occasion.

On the next Sabbath, Jesus called three Apostles aside to a private prayer time. There, high on that hillside, the Christ was transfigured, and Moses and Elijah (representing the Law and the Prophets) appeared, to signify that the Old

Dispensation would be fulfilled in the crucifixion of the Saviour. Peter, James, and John had fallen asleep while Jesus prayed, but when they awoke and saw the glorious scene they understood no more than when in slumber. God the Father spoke from a cloud which descended on the scene.

This is My very own Son who has spoken to all mankind. No one can afford to avoid His words.

Then, on the first day of the week, (in a way, representing the New Dispensation after the symbolic passing of the Old when Moses and Elijah disappeared in the cloud from which God had spoken), Jesus served the multitude at the foot of that mountain. A demonized epileptic boy was such a severe case that the Apostles had been unable to help him. Because Jesus had been fasting and praying, He had the power to immediately perform a cure.

Again the Apostles were reminded that the Messiah would die and not lead an overthrow. But they were so consumed by political dreams that they could think only of the authoritative positions they coveted.

As far as political action is concerned, you are talking to a child when you talk to Me—and My Father. My kingdom will be led by child-like people. The thought of 'governing' is far removed from our service to mankind.

49

So Jesus marched, without hesitation, to His destiny of redemptive death. When Samaritans expressed bigotry toward Him, His Apostles wanted Him to act the Old Testament prophet of judgment.

I do not work in the spirit of Old Testament nationalism. I act solely to serve and save the lives of all men; there is little place in this world for such spiritual direction. A rare father it is who wishes this for his child, so those who follow Me must be ready to forsake the thinking—and approval of family. In this My servant must have a new kind of independent maturity.

In preparation for His arrival at Jerusalem, Jesus sent thirty-five advance teams—seventy men, representing the seventy nations of the world.

Pray for the helpers you urgently need, but don't give any appearance of political or revolutionary design. Associate only with non-political minded people. And don't give any hint of monastic asceticism.

Just dry mankind's tears with the power and love of God. People who reject this approach must be completely shunned. Anquish awaits the religious people who are blindly devoted to political dreams. God has no message but yours of compassion and love.

The evangelist reported great success.

*This spiritual ministry is Satan's doom.
He has no offense or defense to combat
it. The only danger is the temptation,
within you, to spiritual pride.*

The ministry of the Seventy brought overwhelming exultant excitement to the Saviour, for here was proof that love and mercy alone can change the world. He whispered to His Apostles:

*You are witnessing the first display of
the most tightly held secret in the history
of the world.*

An Old Testament Bible scholar asked the Teacher for the road to eternal salvation. The two differed in interpreting the Scriptures.

*Two men who knew all about the true
and living God, totally failed to see their
only tangible opportunity to serve God
when they ignored the needs of an individual absolutely ruined by the blows
of life. But an unprivileged, uninformed
traveler found compassion in his heart,
thus obeying the laws known only
academically by the others.*

Martha of Bethany worked continually to keep a good home of hospitality for the Divine Master, but Mary her sister realized that the duties of life must not forbid the opportunity to carefully listen to the Teacher's message.

Keeping a home should not produce anxiety and weariness, for that can interfere with the enjoyment of the presence of God.

Men wanted to imitate Jesus' prayer life.

Talk to God like this:

' I truly am Your child and

I love Your will and ways.

I trust You one by one for all the passing days.

Please, all my daily sins forgive, for my heart of stone You did replace

With a tender heart of love for all who even my very name disgrace.

Please light my path that I may do my best; give strength to win each moral test.'

Never cease praying for what you want. Prayer is much more than reading a list of desires. If you intently want the full power of the Spirit, the Father will answer that prayer.

The healing of a demonized mute brought charges of demonism against Jesus.

Neither nations nor families can survive internal strife. Since Satan survives, he must not be opposing himself.

I lead God's war against Satan's empire,

and, since you are fighting Me, you must be on the devil's side.

You chose Satan's side FOREVER when you refused to fill your lives with love and compassion for all.

Jesus corrected a woman who wanted to honor His mother, Mary.

All who obey God's will deserve equal honor.

He preached further against the national leaders.

They are wicked. They cannot see beyond their noses and yet they wish to have some visible sign of fire, or something.

Jonah's message of salvation was his 'sign' to the Gentiles. So, My message of love is My 'sign.'

A Gentile queen traveled to hear Solomon's wisdom, but these Pharisees totally reject My great wisdom of love. Those heathen Ninevites recognized truth. These men are willing to live under a little national basket and let the world perish. They were given the opportunity to shine like a glowing lamp for the whole world but they have refused to accept My message which is the light that must first enter the soul of the one who would be a light—and then burn from within, turning the whole person into a lamp for lost mankind.

Eating with some of these Pharisees, who were always washing their hands as a religious duty, Jesus took the occasion to speak.

You are completely superficial in your thinking. You should wash your filthy souls of greed, and then give your possessions away. Then how clean would the world seem to you!

Destruction awaits you; you tithe insincerely—just to buy men's approval. In fact, you are the most unclean element of society, and you defile all who ignorantly have anything to do with you. I refuse to be misunderstood: you who manufacture religious rules are enemies of humanity. You are abhorently evil, just as the murderers of history. But God has placed you at the point of greatest guilt. You have murdered every sincere motivation of life.

The scribes and Pharisees tried to trap Him in some dangerous statement.

Tens of thousands crowded to hear Christ's strong words. But first He warned His Apostles:

You face no greater danger than that of becoming hypocrites—it's something that just grows and grows; you begin thinking

*that you can say one thing in private and
and another in public, and get away with
it—how silly.*

*And hypocrites are always afraid of
one another. Fear only God, He rules
Heaven and Hell. And He loves you dear-
ly. Stand by Me, you'll be honored in
Heaven.*

*Remember, a private small denial of
Me could swell into a fatal full-risen rejection of spiritual reality. Any public crisis
will be a simple matter for those who
have no devious intents.*

Someone asked about a family inheritance.

*I care nothing for that. Greed is the first
sin riches create. A rich farmer with
bursting barns died the fool with a
poverty-stricken soul.*

*My followers must learn victory over
materialism. Food and clothes must not
rule your lives. Birds live and they don't
know how to worry. Worry never accomplished anything. Flowers have dazzling beauty, and it doesn't come from wor-
rying. If you must worry, there is nothing
to what you believe. God WILL take care
of you as you think only of His love and
mercy. Keep absolutely nothing—invest
all in eternal values.*

An attitude of service is what the

Messiah will look for at His revelation—whenever it may be. He will deliver the commission to represent Him to those ready to sacrificially serve. Those religionists who abuse mankind will be discarded—even punished more severely than infidels.

I have brought a new spiritual zeal which will destroy all existing conceptions—and they need to be burned up! After My own suffering, things will be forever changed—how I long to destroy the Old and build the New! There is a sad war which needs to be begun—it shall begin in the homes of Israel. Everyone knows the weather signs—only malignant insincerity keeps this nation from seeing that it is time to change the face of history! But here is a twisted stubbornness which shall cause the loss of all.

The entire nation owes a debt it is going to pay through calamity. Her leaders have shown no repentance during My three years of ministry. They have one more year only!

In a synagogue Sabbath service, Jesus healed a woman whose back was bent with many a painful day. The congregation's leader was angered. Jesus thundered:

Fraud! You treat animals better than humans!

These things I am saying and doing will find lodging in the crevices of men's minds and cover the earth—influencing all mankind.

As Jesus pushed on to Jerusalem, He taught of salvation:

Push through the crowd to the narrow door, before it is locked. There is a deadline. All mankind will be invited— many Israelites will miss everything.

Pharisees sought to frighten Him by mentioning Herod Antipas.

Tell him I will continue My work a little while longer—until it is completed. And I will continue My pace to the holy city. We are both to die in anguish— Jerusalem and I. Weep for Jerusalem.

As a Sabbath dinner guest of an official in the Pharisee fraternity, Jesus healed one of the other visitors. None could criticize His treating men as well as they handled donkeys. Hearing their attitudes He taught them further:

The practice of trying to lie next to the host at a big meal is poor thinking. If you take the end couch you have nowhere to go but up—otherwise you are inviting demotion.

And you host and hostesses, instead of trying to impress your religious friends, impress God by serving meals for the outcasts.

Upon the guests there then dawned the truth that to eat with the poor is to dine with God.

Yes, God Himself gave a great feast, for His 'friends,' Israel, but when many silly excuses were offered, Jehovah turned to the nation's nobodys—then to the world's lowest and lost. But never again shall an invitation be pressed upon the high and mighty.

Thousands thronged Jesus' path to Judea.

Come with Me and you risk being expelled from family—and losing your life. You must be ready and willing to die. But, at such cost, you can build a life of singular majesty, and win a victory of heroic proportions. To build such a life, however, you cannot clutch any relationship or possession—those who do are no good to themselves, to God, or to humanity.

Those with no family, goods, or standing among men crowded to Christ.

You are the 'one lost sheep' I have come to rescue. Heaven loves you.

You are like lost money found. Heaven loves you.

You are like wayward and lost children whose father longs so much to see. When you come to God, confessing your sins, there will be celebrations in Heaven and earth. Some good church people may not appreciate your reception, but the Father's heart will be unspeakably glad.

To His Apostles He continued:

Even crooks escape difficulties and win temporary blessings by showing mercy. Give your money to mercy—souls live forever! If money rules you, you will be spiritually poor. Money never really belongs to the one who is using it—but spiritual wealth is an eternal possession. If you treat money as a real and permanent thing you cannot be My followers.

The greed-filled Pharisees made fun of this appraisal of life.

You are hypocrites seeking the honor of hypocrites. You stink! With John the Baptist things have changed—the outcast 'sinners' are coming home to God. Don't misunderstand, the moral laws of God never change—though you by your selfish, lustful reasonings have sought (for instance) to twist the marriage law—so you can divorce your wives for trivial things each time your hungry eyes see new desires.

Rich and poor are seen differently here on earth, but when death comes another picture emerges. A rich man in Hell cannot buy one drop of water.

Money speaks in time but not in

eternity—no amount of money can build one single bridge from Hell to Heaven.

If rich men, while living, would sincerely listen to the Bible, they would be saved, but apart from honestly facing the Scriptures, they have no hope.

To His Apostles He spoke:

Sometimes people sin because someone has hurt them. How especially horrible for anyone to so injure a poor and weak person. If you are personally injured, scold the offender, hoping he will apologize, so you can forgive and forget. Don't ever give up on this principle! Although it seems difficult, pray for the power to do it. No more than a hired hand doing his job do you deserve special praise for forgiving a brother who apologizes; you can't be My representatives if you can't forever forgive.

On to Jerusalem He trod, through Samaria and Galilee. Ten lepers prayed for cleansing and received it, but only one, a Samaritan, expressed thanks.

Where are the nine Israelites?

Pharisees sarcastically asked about His 'kingdom.'

It's not that kind of kingdom. It's whenever and wherever God lives with a man.

60

Then to His Apostles:

Remember, My kingdom comes not with pomp, yet will be as clear as day.

But first I must be killed by these Pharisees.

Like Noah's world, this nation will be destroyed in an unexpected judgment.

My followers must not try to defend her—there is nothing worth saving. Lose your identity as Israelites, and you will have won a greater identity for which Israel was created. The nation will be divided on this issue—along very personal lines.

Those who choose nationalistic racism are like vultures choosing a corpse.

To self-righteous hypocrites He spoke.

Watch two men go to the house of God. One looks so good and the other everyone knows to be a scoundrel—and he knows it too. This makes him wiser than the 'upright' man, and makes it possible for him to be born again.

Babies were brought for Jesus' touch.

Yes, bring them to Me, never interfere with children—this is a perfect picture of how all people must approach God.

A young man with position in Israel wanted to be saved.

You call all rabbis 'good,' when only God is. They have taught you your obligations. The one thing they haven't taught you is to give all your wealth to the needy.

He was affluent and greedy.

So hard it is for rich people to be saved that to all human understanding it is impossible.

The Apostles had forsaken all.

I promise you, for this life, more than enough emotional rest, love, and satisfaction to compensate for any sacrifice. And you will win eternally.

Again He spoke privately to the Apostles about His imminent death and resurrection, but they had no comprehension—it seemed so impossible.

They approached Jericho. The great commotion caused a blind beggar to inquire, then beg for his vision. As Jesus entered the 'City of Palm Trees,' the man with new sight was with Him.

In that resort city lived a rich tax-gatherer. Zaccheus, diminuitive but determined, climbed a sycamore fig tree to be able to see Jesus over the throng.

I see you, come quickly, I'll visit your home.

By so receiving Christ, Zaccheus was born again. It was an amazing thing that Jesus would go home with such a big crook. But regenerated Zaccheus was truly a new man, and he proved it.

This is just the kind of lost Israelite whom I, the Messiah, have come to find—and to give salvation to!

The Apostles and others still thought they were marching to Jerusalem for a take-over.

I will not receive My kingdom in Jersualem, but like the Herods who went to Rome to obtain their kingdom grants, (one of them, Archaelaus, from right here in Jericho) I am going to ascend to My Father's throne-room to be crowned.

But, before My departure, I am leaving with a few people seemingly small deposits of trust, to be managed and increased for me. Since My kingdom is world-wide, every man's subjection or rebellion while I am away will be noted. When I return to reward My servants who were with Me before the coronation, I will see how they passed the test of service. Those who multiply My investment will be honored, and those who are unagressive in My work will be ashamed.

In My kingdom, each man has equal opportunity for success and advancement

> *since anyone can be humble, sincere, lov-*
> *ing and fearless. In that Day of Reward*
> *My enemies shall be punished.*

Jerusalem was at hand, and, nearby was a village in which was an untamed donkey, just waiting for Jesus' ride into the city.

The throng of disciples who had been walking with Jesus praised and shouted as He neared the crest of Olivet. The cheers were wildly enthusiastic, as they represented enormous reserves of pent-up feelings. Jesus, too, was filled with overflowing emotion.

> *I weep, for you cannot see the only*
> *route of peace. You are doomed to die in*
> *awful war—because you could not see.*

In the Temple He was angry with the merchant-priests.

> *Out! You have murdered* PRAYER *and*
> *enthroned* GREED.

The Temple authorities asked Jesus for His credentials.

> *Where did John the Baptist get his*
> *authority?*

No one could afford to criticize John.

> *Israel has long been God's garden. The*
> *prophets have been God's inspectors—*
> *and all have been mistreated. Now I,*
> *God's son and heir, shall be killed by you*

64

officials of the divine vineyard. God will remove you and choose others.

They got the point of this parable.

In a few moments the Temple choirs will be singing the 'Hallel,' which, in reality, tells of your rejection of Me, and of My judgment upon you.

Infiltrators followed Jesus about, hoping to bait Him into expressing some treason against Rome, so that the Empire would have to execute Him.

The government mints money, so it deserves taxes. God creates souls, so the conscience belongs to Him.

The worldly-minded Sadducees, who rejected the supernatural, asked about a woman who was widowed seven times.

This life is physical. There is another world of immortality—in which marriage is not needed, for births are unnecessary seeing that the resurrected shall never die.

The 'Bible teachers' were glad to see the secularists put down so effectively.

Since a son is never above his father, how can the Christ be ruler over King David, whom every Israelite agrees is the 'Father' of Messiah? Only His resurrection, proving His deity, can make that possible. You scribes, who believe in resurrection, should accept My deity.

All could hear as Jesus condemned the 'Bible teachers' also.

They are dangerous hypocrites— stealing and praying.

While in the Temple, Jesus noted a destitute woman who was giving God her all—plus a little money.

The great wealth invested in this Temple by the rich will perish with it in its day of destruction.

Beware of sign-seekers, date-setters, and interpreters of foreboding current events. Before anything occurs which could be taken as a sign, there is much work and suffering for you. You will preach truths to shake the world. You will be condemned to death by intimate family members. Show courage and patience in the face of death, and you will survive.

Then, when Rome surrounds Jerusalem, forsake the city. Nothing will save Jerusalem. I feel such pain for the women and mothers of that day. All the world's great cities will one day be destroyed, too. Their ruin will be cataclysmic and frightening. That is when I will personally return—redeeming all creation!

Again, don't worry about false alarms; the seige of Jerusalem and the destruction of Gentile cities shall occur before this age is ended. You can count on these words.

Now, on the other hand, My people must not grow indifferent to My imminent return. Stay awake and close to God—the only way to avoid disaster.

Each day, thousands thronged Him in the Temple to hear His matchless words.

As the week wore on, the burgeoning crowds more and more frightened the religious leaders. Judas, an apostle (really of Satan), offered to help find a quiet way to kill Jesus—for money.

On the fifth day of Passover week each household killed a lamb and had a solemn feast, eating also flat, yeastless bread. Jesus had safely (secretly) arranged a site for Himself and the Twelve.

I did not want to miss this one opportunity to eat a Passover meal together. We will not meet again this way until My new churches spread the communion meal. Then remember, the bread is the reminder of My sufferings for My churches, the wine is the reminder of the new birth given each believer because I am willing to shed My blood. Even now, treason is at our table.

From the ensuing argument over who could possibly betray the Christ, the Apostles entered debate over who was the best Apostle, most likely to be chief in authority.

There is a chain of command in the Roman empire, but never among My people. There are 'big shots' and 'little people' in the world, but never at My table. I am your slave, so who could be important sitting at the meal? As the congregation meets at the Table of Communion, always remember that I am there serving, and that all of you are being honored by Me as though you were kings.

Peter, you, especially, must now discover your weaknesses, before you become a leader. You don't know how weak you are—you have not been tested in hostile surroundings.

All of you can remember how easy it was to evangelize among so many friendly people when I was hailed as the great Teacher and Healer, but now you must take every precaution necessary for life and defense, for you are entering a very dangerous world in which I will be regarded as a convicted criminal, just as Isaiah predicted.

They thought that, finally, He might be planning the military-like takeover which so many wanted.

Let's drop the subject for now.

As so often before, Jesus then retired to His garden of prayer. He urged the Apostles to pray for victory over cowardice, then He prayed to the Father for any possible delivery from the Cross.

But I WILL do Thy will.

As tension mounted within His emotions, large clots of red sweat fell from His face.

Only through much prayer did He find the strength to face the death of a disgraced preacher.

The Apostles were asleep (it was one o'clock in the morning).

If I must so agonize in prayer, how can you meet your tests by sleeping?

Judas came with his kiss.

The Apostles thought it now time to use the swords in the offensive action they had mistakenly thought that Jesus had earlier instructed. Jesus healed the one wound inflicted.

Never do that again!

Then the Saviour looked at the religious rulers and their police.

Cowards! Your best hour is the depth of night.

With his enemies now in charge, Jesus' Apostles surrendered to fear. After repeated

69

betrayals by Peter, his Lord's gaze brought burning tears.

The Saviour was blindfolded, beaten, and ridiculed. About 5:00 A.M. an irregular religious trial was conducted.

> You have pre-judged; nothing I might say could change your minds. But soon I will have all the power in the universe. As you have said, I am God's Son.

This was taken as a confession deserving of death.

They hurried off to Pilate to obtain the death sentence. By 5:30 A.M. Pilate had shuffled Him to Herod, ruler of Galilee, who was visiting the city.

Flippant, curious Herod received not a word from Jesus. In that palace the Lord was accused and humiliated, and was sent away, wearing elegant clothing of purple, white, and scarlet. To Herod it was great sport.

Pilate reassembled the clerics and sought to dissuade them of their goal. But they valued a murderer above Jesus and continued their litany of death. The issue was carried by the mob's orchestrated screams of hate.

Jesus was substituted for the murderer who was scheduled to die.

A traveler (later to become a well-known believer) bore the death timber behind Jesus. It was now after seven o'clock and many of the Teacher's students had congregated as a mourner's procession, among them many women—especially pitied by the Master.

Oh, it is you and your babies who face such suffering as the result of your blind rulers, and there is nothing anyone can do but weep, and weep and weep. The Romans do not hate Me but they will slaughter you with raging vengeance.

By nine o'clock He had been nailed and raised between two convicts by the Roman soldiers.

Father, I pray for these poor ignorant sinners.

Herod's royal raiment became the booty of the soldiers, who joined priests and acolytes in bitter derision. But no one dared touch the ironic placard of praise nailed above His head.

The dying criminals were divided in their attitude toward the Saviour of the world. One believed, as best he could.

Today, with Me, your soul will rest in peace.

It was night at noon, but, in this darkness, the presence of God was being opened for every man, woman, boy, and girl—and Jesus led the way.

The commanding soldier could not restrain

his admiration for such a Man. The drama of the moment overcame the crowd, so recently wild with hate.

The women who had financed Jesus' ministry did not forsake Him in His death.

One of the rulers had not concurred in the night's proceedings, and now, as a believer, cared for the body of Jesus. By this time, it was 5 P.M., and Saturday, the High Passover Sabbath was to begin at six. Those women supporters began readying spices to kill the odor of decay until only bones would be left to be buried in an urn.

Loyal Jews did not work on Saturdays, so it was early in the dawn of Sunday's sunrise that they came with the spices. The hillside tomb was open, and two angels announced the resurrection! The women reported to the Apostles and disciples, who were not prepared to believe any such story.

Peter suddenly ran to the tomb site, peeped through the little window, and left, scratching his head.

Two disciples, making the seven mile walk to their home in Emmaus were joined by a Stranger on the road. They explained to Him all the events of the preceeding week.

It is hard to believe people can be so simple! How could you have missed all the Old Testament predictions about

Christ? Let Me remind you, from Genesis to Malachi, of the many passages referring to the shedding of His blood and of the resurrection of His body.

They prayed the Holy Stranger to abide with them, for fast was falling the evening darkness. As they fellowshipped, it dawned on them that this was Jesus! They ran the seven miles back to Jerusalem to tell their story to the Eleven. Jesus suddenly appeared.

Why this fear, why do you assume I am a ghost? Look at Me, touch Me. Since you still think I am a spirit, give Me some food to devour—a ghost certainly can not eat food.

This is what I have been teaching you from the Bible. Now it is time for you to comprehend those Scriptures which foretell the death and resurrection of Messiah, and for the proclaiming of free salvation to all the peoples of the world. You are seeing it all come true.

Wait right here in this city for the 'baptism' of power from Heaven.

They all walked with Jesus to Bethany by the Mount of Olives. Stretching His hands over them, and speaking a benediction, He visibly ascended out of their sight. They then carried their great joy back to the Temple, where they daily glorified God for all He had done.

John

Prologue

At the heart of the universe is the light of infinite love and truth.

Jesus is that Light and each man is born with enough knowledge stamped upon his conscience to enable him to recognize Jesus as true God.

John the Baptist announced that the Light had reached mankind. In general, Gentiles ignored the Light and Jews rejected Him, but Christ created a new church out of the many individuals who came to His light.

━━━━━━━━━━━━━━━━━━━━━━━

John the Baptist was just a forerunner preparing the Jews for Christ and honoring Jesus as God's gift of salvation and eternal Son. He also provided the first disciples for Jesus, John (author of this Gospel), Andrew, Peter, Philip, and Nathanael. They, too, all confessed the deity of Jesus.

Jesus and these disciples attended a wedding

at which the new Prophet performed His first miracle—turning water into wine. After visiting Capernaum, He went to Jerusalem for the Passover—and the formal opening of His ministry. In His first act He drove the money-changers out of the Temple.

There the Saviour also spoke of His resurrection (yet four years in the future) and worked many miracles, quietly.

A Temple official made a personal inquiry, and was instructed by the Teacher to be 'born again.'

You, though already a religious man, must confess, as men do in baptism, that you are no different from all the ignorant and ungodly in that you, too, need forgiveness and a new life,

Being born again is just as simple—and mysterious—as an evening breeze, and has happened many times. You must grasp this before you can understand anything further.

The simplest act of faith brings eternal life, for God has given Himself, in His eternal Son, to do the suffering and pay the price to save you—and anyone in the world. No one has hope who rejects this Light.

Soon, Jesus' fame surpassed that of John the Baptist. John was pleased. He had never claimed to be Messiah, just the 'friend of the groom.' He preached Jesus as having come from Heaven, with power knowing no limits— the Saviour of men.

Jesus left Judea and brewing controversies about His success. Traveling through Samaria, He stopped and talked with a lonely woman at a well-side. She chatted religion, though, in fact, she was quite a 'sinner.' The Saviour kindly dealt with her.

The true God is everywhere and will meet you anywhere. He knows everything about you and loves you still.

She accepted Christ as her Saviour, was born again, and immediately began to evangelize her city.

Jesus' disciples did not fully comprehend.

There are, right now, many cities to evangelize. The rewards are great and the work is not as difficult as it may seem.

There was a mighty revival in Samaria. After leaving that area Jesus was welcomed in Galilee. At Cana, a man from Capernaum pleaded for the healing of his little boy (who remained in Capernaum). Jesus responded immediately, thus performing a second miracle at Cana.

Returning to Judea and Jerusalem, Jesus visited Bethesda Spring where lay many paralytics. He healed the most distressing case. Because it was a Sabbath, the Temple authorities raged and began efforts to kill Him. Their plots were further fired by Jesus' assertion of His deity.

> I do what My Father taught Me. He raises the dead; I heal this paralytic. To honor the Father you must honor me; do this and you have eternal life. I have all authority.

> At the resurrection those who have believed on Me will be without any condemnation—proof that I am from God.

> I have four witnesses: first, John the Baptist; second, My mighty works; third, the Father (through the Holy Spirit); and fourth, the Scriptures themselves.

> But you miss Scripture's testimony because you do not read in an attitude of love. You are only interested in the workings and interrelationships of your own little group. So it is impossible for you to have an objective approach to the Bible.

Two years after Jesus opened His ministry on a Passover in Jerusalem, He was at a remote mountain on the west coast of the Sea of Galilee. Some twenty thousand had followed Him there. For food there was only a boy's lunch. The Saviour organized the crowd and broke the bread into even more than was needed.

With such power He could have been the king of any land!

On the night of that miracle Jesus walked on the stormy sea to guide His disciples to their port.

The next day the crowd followed to Capernaum in quest of their 'leader.' Jesus addressed them in the synagogue.

You are not filled with compassion, but with nationalistic greed.

Believe on Me as compassionate Saviour. I am not building a nation, but saving a world—one person at a time. This is the Father's plan.

(But Jesus' audience was extremely nationalistic and racially oriented.)

If you can not understand this devotion to all men, you can not comprehend Me. My Father and I are doing something larger than any nation.

Even the disciples had difficulty with these words.

Someday you will understand—after the ascension; that is, those of you who have truly been born again.

Most of the crowd forsook Him. (And one of

79

His closest 'friends' was to betray Him.)

Hatred fermented throughout Judea. James and Jesus' other brothers (in unbelief) dared Him to face that area head-on.

Any time is good enough for your limited thoughts, but My mission requires the precise moment.

Then Jesus secretly left Galilee for a September holy week in Jerusalem. The authorities were looking for Him, but He waited several days to begin teaching.

I teach God's word and any sincere man can understand it.

If you love God's Law, why do you want to murder Me?

I astounded you by healing that paralytic at Bethesda Pool on a Sabbath. And yet you also feel you must do certain things on the Sabbath. Can't you see the contradiction?

Some were surprised that Jesus was permitted to speak so boldly. When He even more forcibly declared His deity, an arrest was ordered and attempted.

Somehow He stopped them with His words.

Not yet! I have more to do before I return to Heaven—where you will never go.

At the climax of the celebrations Jesus loudly interrupted an impressive water-pouring ceremony.

I will satisfy the thirsty, and My followers will have water for the world.

This utterance produced consternation and confusion. The Temple guards simply could not touch Him for the majesty of His words. The authorities cursed the 'ignorant' Galileans who were crowding the Temple and cheering Jesus. Nicodemus, the ruler who had heard Him explain being born again, argued against an arrest.

The following day, as Jesus taught, members of the bigoted Pharisee fraternity broke through the crowd, bringing an adulterous woman to be 'judged' by Jesus.

Let spotless men punish this soiled woman.

Then Jesus was left standing alone with the fallen woman as the surrounding crowd looked on.

Go. As a born-again woman, go.

After this He addressed the authorities of Jewry.

I give light to men, and My followers will light the world.

You Pharisees share none of My thinking—nor I yours.

You could hear the Father's voice if you would only listen to me.

(The shock of His powerful words continued to protect Him.)

I will return to Heaven—a place you will never see because you deny My deity.

I continue to tell you that I am God's Son. After you kill Me you will know more.

To the many who accepted those words He taught further.

Think continually about My words; the truth will penetrate and set you free.

The unbelievers were warned.

Sinners are slaves. Slaves can be sold— or freed—by the heir. So I am freeing slaves.

You claim to be Abraham's sons, but you are someone else's sons—and you are not children of God!

You know not God's vocabulary of love because you think the murderous thoughts of your father, the devil!

They called Him a demonized Samaritan.

But I can rescue from death.

Now they *knew* He was crazy. But Jesus

merely reinforced His astounding claims of deity. And they sought to kill Him.

As Jesus left the Temple He was asked about a man born blind.

No one is to be blamed, this misery is love's opportunity. I am here to give sight to a blind world.

The healed blind man created quite a stir. The Pharisees, at first confused over the Sabbath-day miracle, upon confirming it, expelled the man from his Jewish church simply because he was happy he had been given sight on Moses' holy day. Jesus offered him a new fellowship, and he accepted.

(These events illustrate which blindness is punishment for sin.)

You hypocrites and your churches are blind because of the awful immoral sin of insincerity.

I am straightforward and open. Even blind men, who are not hypocrites, will leave your crowd to follow Me. They then enter a new spiritual fellowship of eternal meaningful life and spiritual sight. Their new churches are to be built at the expense of My own blood. As this blind man has come to Me from Israel, so others will come to Me from many nations —after I give My life and rise again.

All the Jewish leaders would have, then and there, rejected Him—but He really *had* healed that blind man.

On a day in late December Jesus again expounded this theme in the Temple.

Any sincere man can examine My words and My miracles. He will come into My church and no one will be able to expel him—for I am God.

For this the Jewish leaders would have thrown Him into a ditch and dropped boulders on Him.

Why are you unwilling to make decisions based upon Scripture and clear evidence?

Jesus escaped into Perea, east of the Jordan, where many of John the Baptist's followers accepted Him.

Lazarus, a devoted follower who lived near Jerusalem, became seriously ill, but the Saviour did not rush to him.

Jesus' Galilean disciples, afraid of the Judean Jews, urged Him not to go at all.

Don't worry, My steps are sure. Theirs are unsure because they are blind. My friend is dead, but I will awaken him.

Arriving in Bethany where the body was entombed, Jesus found the two distraught sisters—and Jewish friends offering comfort.

Tears flowed down His face and people heard His sobs of grief.

With absolute confidence in the Father and in prayer, Jesus ordered the tomb opened.

Friend, I am calling!

Lazarus came up the short stairwell into the sunlight. This caused many of the Jews to accept Jesus as the Son of God. Others alerted the Jerusalem authorities, who then convened their Council. Some of them feared that Jesus would eventually bring Rome's crushing fist upon the Jews.

The Chief Priest resolved to kill Jesus before He could antagonize the Empire. (He had no idea how prophetic were his words concerning *one man* dying to spare *a nation*—for Jesus was to die for *His church* of *many nations*.)

Jesus retreated to a little village as many from all the countryside arrived in Jerusalem for Passover. Everyone wondered about Jesus' plans—there was a general alert for His arrest.

On the Saturday night before the final preparations for Passover, Jesus was in Bethany with Lazarus and his sisters having dinner.

When Mary washed Jesus' feet with expensive perfume, the treasurer of the Twelve objected, having a better use—himself.

Jerusalem Jews flocked to Bethany to see Jesus and Lazarus. The Council planned death for both.

85

When word of Jesus' presence reached the Jews from the countryside, they lined His path into Jerusalem. His march into the City of David on that Sunday was dramatic, but no one was aware of how profound was its significance. Primarily on these people's minds was the raising of Lazarus from the dead.

The Council feared they had not been able to act fast enough.

Non-Jewish visitors from distant lands sought to have an interview with Jesus.

The nations will know Me. The death now upon Me will take My presence to all lands, for My followers will sacrifice their personal ambitions in order to take My message to the world. They will have all authority and power. My death is the seed that must be planted.

In this stupendous moment, God the Father audibly confirmed these promises of Jesus.

This is the victory of humanity. My Cross will be the rallying point of mankind. Believe what you see and hear today and you will not miss any of the unfolding truth.

Most of Jerusalem's Jews believed nothing He said. And those who did accept Him were cowardly silent, so as not to be expelled from their congregations (synagogues).

To believe Me is to trust God; to see Me is to look upon God. I am God's light come to take you from the darkness of enslaving religion. Someday you will have to explain why you did not want to be rescued from slavery and given eternal freedom.

Thursday night before the Saturday Passover, Jesus knew that it was His time to die.

Judas also knew.

Alone with His apostles at the Passover meal, the Saviour tied a long towel around His waist and knelt behind each reclining apostle to wash their feet as they ate.

You cannot be My follower unless you permit Me to be your Servant, for this is at the heart of My teachings. The leader must serve the follower, and each one must be a leader. You are not greater than I, any more than is a messenger greater than the one sending the message. You will find happiness when you imitate Me in this.

I am predicting an imminent betrayal by one of you. But the rest of you will be My messengers with all My personal authority—and humility.

With anguish of mind Jesus identified (for Peter and John) the trusted treasurer, Judas, as the betrayer.

Judas arose and left, joining the night which had fallen during the meal.

Now I approach the hour when I exalt God the Father and He exalts Me. I am going to die and leave you—like the untimely death of a parent. Remember, if you show love for one another, you will prove to all that you are My children.

We will be together again—but now I must suffer alone. Do not worry about the sorrows of life. In Heaven we will see the tangles untied. I will bring you to Heaven.

The road to Heaven is Truth—the light that gives life. I am all this for you. Truth is of My Father; to know My truth is to know My Father. This is how the Father is known.

There is no limit to what the Father and I will do for and through you if you will adopt this truth and pray with the authority of My name.

Love Me by loving one another.

The Holy Spirit will come as your Comforter. You will not be orphaned. Through Him I will be in you. You will have Father, Son, and Holy Spirit.

Love Me by loving one another.

Love is our secret, known only by those who hear My words and listen to the Holy Spirit.

Perfect peace is yours. It is greater than all the storms of life. Be happy for Me as I go to My Father who will comfort and refresh Me. Satan has no power over Me; I die in obedience to My Father's plan.

Now walk with Me to the garden of prayer.

Through Me you will produce, as a branch in a grapevine. My Father, as a gardener, has trimmed the dead twigs from you as you received My teachings. Draw productive strength from this knowledge. Ignore it and you will be fruitless. I will give you as much fruit as you ask for.

Love Me by loving one another.

I will fill your cup of joy with the joy I have in serving mankind. I die for you My friends: I have chosen to tell you all and to give you unlimited promises for power in service.

Love Me by loving one another.

There is enough hate in this world; I have chosen you to love—and this will cause men to hate you as they have Me. Hateful men do not know God. I have shown them how to love, and they hate even more. I did miracles no other man has ever done and they hate Me more. Strong is their desire to rule men. But nothing can destroy My ministry of love.

Congregations of hate will be too small for you; their officials will kill you. You must know these things now even though your interest in them is low and you are filled with sadness.

The Holy Spirit will bring greater things. He will show everyone the crimes of human depravity displayed in all men who want to be served by men—as those who hate and kill the One who has preached that all men must serve one another.

The Holy Spirit will also open up everything to you. You will be enabled to see My truth much more clearly.

The coming of the Comforter will turn sadness into song. Something new will be born: there will be a church of overflowing happiness. It will be a new day of prayer and clearer understanding of each born-again person's direct relationship to the Father.

Though you think you understand now, you will soon flee, leaving Me to be humiliated alone. But, in My death, I defeat worldly authorities and you can forever celebrate the victory.

Jesus stopped along the path to Gethsemane and prayed.

Father, lift Me high among men.

In My death may My work be crowned so that I bring Your presence to men all over the earth.

I have done everything I can. Men must now see My deity.

I have fully instructed My Apostles. They are ready. Keep them close to You and Me. Give them a unity unlike men's slavish systems: may they all serve one another.

Guard them from becoming cultish recluses. Make their difference the uniqueness of their message as they take Your compassion and love among men— just as I have done.

I pray this not for My apostles alone: may all believers have the humble devotion to sacrificial service which I have illustrated among men.

Bring all My followers to Heaven.

Men who wish to own and use one another can not comprehend Me; but My Apostles have accepted Our call to loving service, and I have told them all about it. Speed them.

Into a wooded garden the Master went, with His students.

Judas, with Temple policemen, found Him there.

The Saviour's voice was calm, and His presence overpowering.

He was willing to suffer shame, disgrace, and death.

They tied His arms to His sides and took Him to the man who sat at the top of the religious hierarchy.

(Apostles Peter and John had quietly found their way there. And Peter was so afraid.)

I spread My thought in the sunlight;
why question Me in the shadows!

A policeman slapped Him.

This you do for you have nothing to
say.

They took Him to the second highest.

(And Peter was so afraid.)

They took Him to the civil governor; he was the only one who could crucify.

Jesus answered Pilate, the governor.

How can you judge Me with no direct
knowledge?

I rule a kingdom no sword can touch.
It is the Empire of Truth.

Pilate was afraid to learn truth.

A crowd had been whipped to frenzied hate.

Pilate brutalized Jesus and let Him be mocked and humiliated. He thought he had proven the Galilean to be no threat to anyone.

But the functionaries of the religious hierarchy knew that He was their mortal threat.

When Pilate heard that Jesus claimed deity, he urgently begged Him to explain.

I am not trying to overthrow you, Pilate. But I will destroy this immoral, illegal religious tyranny.

Pilate sought to let Him go, but he feared the Jews' threat of accusations to Rome. In the early dawn he tried to convince the Jews that Jesus was not dangerous. But the oppressive religious bosses knew that He was their greatest danger. Pilate could not refuse them.

Jesus was nailed to an old rugged cross.

Pilate honored Him with dramatic words of ageless significance, but too little, and too late, for his own soul.

Roman soldiers clothed themselves in Jesus' garments—but not in His peace.

Three Marys watched Him die. Since His brothers were not yet believers, He commissioned the Apostle John to care for His mother.

With sour wine the soldiers moistened His parched lips and swollen mouth. He then gave His final triumphant cry.

Men stared at an erupting gash slashed in His side.

Two timid followers cared for the corpse of Christ and laid Him in a borrowed tomb.

Jesus arose very early on that first Sunday morning.

Peter and John, and Mary Magdalene, could grasp only that He was not in the tomb.

Mary's tears of grief and perplexity were dried when He called her name.

Go tell My Apostles.

On Sunday evening, as a fearful church met behind locked doors, Jesus came—bringing security.

Perfect tranquility is yours—look at My wounds.

You have nothing to fear—the Father who raised Me from death will guide you on your mission.

He will give your words such power they will be the difference in men's eternal destinies.

The next Sunday, doubting Thomas, who would accept nothing but first-hand proof, touched the wounds, and shouted his faith.

It is not necessary to see and feel in order to have faith.

(Yes, this little book tells enough to produce life-giving faith in anyone.)

The third time Jesus appeared to all the Eleven was when He again ministered in Galilee, by the sea. It was time to make the final transformation of His fishermen Apostles into the great shepherds of the nations. He prepared and ate with them a breakfast of rededication.

Though I should ask a thousand questions, they would all be the same: Do you love Me? If your heart is full of 'Yes' then I have only one command: take the Bread of Life to every hungry soul around the world—throughout all time.

In your youthful dreams you planned your own lives; now as servants of souls you will sacrifice and suffer.

I alone will be the Lord of each individual servant.

I, the Apostle John, was an eye-witness to everything I have told you about in this book— from John the Baptist to these final scenes. I could never have written all that I saw and heard, and there is not space to explain the infinite significance of each.

Acts

After Jesus' crucifixion, He met with the Apostles several times, instructing them to expect something marvelous and overwhelming.

No, not a political revolution, but a spiritual revival.

Jesus then ascended into Heaven. The believers began an extended prayer conference, in which they also cared for organizational matters, such as selecting a new apostle.

Ten days after Jesus returned to Heaven, the regular morning prayer meeting was visited by the Holy Spirit with the sound of a cyclone, which attracted thousands of visiting pilgrims. They were amazed to hear their own languages being miraculously spoken by uneducated men.

Peter preached to the huge crowd in the commonly known Greek tongue.

Prophecy is being fulfilled before your very eyes. The entire human race is to be blessed. This is all of immense importance.

God allowed you Israelites to kill Jesus, then He raised Him from the dead.

King David wrote of Jesus and His resurrection.

Jesus now has great authority in Heaven. He, Himself, has sent the Holy Spirit, and you have heard His arrival.

AND THIS IS THE MESSIAH YOU CRUCIFIED!

Many were convicted, and clearly confessed Jesus as Lord and Saviour.

After Peter concluded his sermon, three thousand joined the church in Jerusalem. There was a wonderful spirit of love in the church.

Later, two apostles, arriving at the Temple for a daily afternoon prayer meeting, responded to a crippled beggar by healing him. This brought a crowd, and again Peter preached.

The God of our fathers has honored Jesus by healing this well known cripple.

You rejected and killed Jesus. But we have seen Him alive. His very name brought this healing.

You can repent and enjoy all of God's blessings promised of old—and you can be a blessing to the whole world.

The Temple rulers arrested Peter and John, but many Jews had been born again. At the official inquiry, on the following day, Peter addressed the very men who had condemned Christ.

Make no mistake, my power and authority is Jesus of Nazareth Himself— the One whom you discarded.

The perplexed council tried to frighten them, but the apostles accepted no intimidation.

The church prayed for more boldness, and all were again filled with the Holy Spirit—and the building actually shook.

The followers of Jesus in that congregation loved each other greatly.

A couple tried to play a game of deceit in the church. They did not know that to lie to the church is to lie to God. Both of the deceivers were struck dead, to the awe of many.

Because the Temple continued to be the site of great Gospel gatherings, the apostles were again arrested and jailed. But an angel opened the prison and ordered them back to the Temple to preach.

A full hearing was convened, and when the apostles were once again found, the High Priest began his accusations. When the apostles vowed to disobey any order to cease preaching, the death penalty was mentioned. Only the intervention of a moderate voice on the Council spared them. However, they did not escape being flogged. But they left with great happiness in

99

their hearts, and Christ their conversation.

Demands of church administration required the election of seven deacons—and at a good time, for evangelism was swelling the size of the church.

Stephen, one of the seven chosen to serve, had the power of an apostle. Fanatics bitterly opposed him, causing his arrest. He addressed the Jewish Council.

Abraham answered God's call. God promised him a land, and a family (Israel). That family, even in its infancy, had treachery and jealousy within it, which led to its enslavement.

But God's grace protected them in Egypt.

Then, Moses was given. And his initial efforts to rescue the Israelites were rebuffed. But God later called, encouraged, and empowered him to save the nation.

IT WAS MOSES HIMSELF WHO PREDICTED ANOTHER GREAT LEADER.

But Israelites still opposed Moses, and after the Exodus, they worshipped like pagans for forty years, even though they had a divine Tabernacle of true worship.

Later, Solomon built the Temple. But God clearly said that He could not be confined in it.

This Council is just like those treacherous and apostate elements forever plaguing Israel. YOU EVEN KILLED THE MESSIAH!

Caiaphas and his Council boiled with rage. They personally dragged Stephen to a ravine, where they dropped huge stones on him. Stephen died with radiant joy, and forgiveness for his murderers on his lips. Jesus welcomed him to Heaven.

Saul (Paul), a Pharisee, and member of the Sanhedrin Council, about thirty-six years of age, was especially glad to see Stephen die. He soon helped begin a general persecution to rid Jerusalem of 'the Jesus Way.'

Many church members fled the Holy City, preaching on their way. Philip, another of the deacons, preached with great success in Samaria. Even the most prominent figure in that city, a magician, was converted. Peter and John came down from Jerusalem, and the new believers were baptized in the Holy Spirit. Seeing this, the former sorcerer sought to purchase apostolic authority. When totally repudiated, he melted in repentance.

As Peter and John preached their way to Jerusalem, God led Philip to a desert road-side, where he came across the Treasurer of Ethiopia. This man loved the Old Testament, but did not understand it. When Philip explained the

Gospel, the Ethiopian was born again, and baptized. Philip then preached his way to Caesarea, the Roman capital of Judea.

Saul continued building fires of persecution.

But Jesus personally stopped him, and Saul was born again. He was led, blinded, into the ancient Syrian city of Damascus, where God had given one believer apostolic authority to impart the 'baptism' of the Spirit. Saul was baptized, received his sight, and soon began preaching the Gospel in the city's synagogue.

He made a big impact in Damascus, and was soon himself the object of a death plot. Friends spirited him away to safety, over the city wall, in a basket

In Jerusalem, he could at first make no friends among the believers—except for Barnabas, a generous-minded man from Cyprus. Barnabas removed the church's fears of Saul.

Here, too, Saul's life fell in danger to the Jews, and believers whisked him away—now to his home, Tarsus, in Asia Minor (Turkey).

The first big persecution of believers had ended. Peter, the prominent apostle, traveled about strengthening the churches, healing the sick, and raising the dead.

In Caesarea, a Roman officer desired to be saved, and Peter, who was just down the coast in Joppa, was the one God chose to lead this

Gentile to Christ. But even Jesus' church had not yet been opened directly to non-Jews. It was difficult for Peter to accept such a drastic change, but he did go to Caesarea, as God indicated. There, he found a group of Gentiles eager to hear God's message.

He forced himself beyond his fears, and, having clearly seen God's will, preached the Gospel to them. Immediately, they gave a positive response, believing the Gospel. They were born again, and received the Holy Spirit—without becoming Jewish converts, and even before they were baptized.

The Jerusalem believers were indignant over Peter's actions, but when he explained God's will, rehearsed the facts and told how the Spirit honored those Gentiles, the church seemed to fully understand.

The believers scattered by the persecution had been preaching only to Jews, but now men traveling from Jerusalem to Cyprus through Syria preached to and won many Gentiles. Open-minded Barnabas was sent to Antioch to assist with that great mixed congregation. He went on to Asia Minor to enlist the help of his old friend, Saul, who had been living there in obscurity for the past eight years.

It was at Antioch that terms such as 'Jew,' 'Greek,' 'proselyte,' 'Gentile,' 'clean,' and 'unclean' were all replaced by one new description—'Christian.'

When a Christian prophet from Jerusalem predicted a famine, the Antioch church appointed Barnabas and Saul to deliver contributions for the Christians of Jerusalem.

About that time, in Jerusalem, the grandson of Herod the Great started a new persecution. He killed Peter's brother-in-law James (not the James who was the pastor), and planned Peter's execution.

The Jersualem church prayed.

An angel led Peter out of prison, and the Apostle found his way to the prayer meeting.

The church could not believe so great an answer to prayer.

Herod Agrippa killed the sixteen prison guards, and then busied himself with other matters; but his ungodly arrogance brought him an awful death.

Barnabas and Paul made their trip to Jerusalem, returning to Antioch with Mark, a relative of Barnabas. Once back, the Holy Spirit burdened them to launch a missionary trip.

The three preached first in Salamis, Cyprus. At Paphos, Sergius Paulus, the widely-read governor, wished to hear the Gospel, but a Jewish magician attempted to prevent his conversion. Great powers then displayed themselves in Saul, Sergius Paulus was born again, and 'Paul' became Saul's name.

The three men sailed to Perga in Asia Minor (Turkey), where the young Mark dropped out.

Barnabas and Paul traveled northward to Antioch, Psidia, in the highland interior. In its synagogue, Paul's prominence was evidenced in his bold preaching.

The God of Hebrew history, who sent John the Baptist, now sends me with the message of salvation.

Israel's blind leaders killed Messiah.

But He lives!

We bring the Gospel promised of old.

Through faith in Jesus there is forgiveness of sins.

Be careful not to choose blindness.

The Gentiles asked to hear more. Within a week the city was stirred with interest, but the Jews were stirred with anger.

The apostles renounced the favored position of Judiasm and turned directly to the Gentiles, who responded by accepting Christ—and spreading the Gospel. At this, the Jews expelled the apostles, who, in turn, designated them as heathen.

In the next city, Iconium, many were saved, but unbelieving Jewish zealots caused much trouble, spreading lies the entire length of the apostles' protracted stay. Finally, Paul and Barnabas had to flee for their lives.

At Lystra, when Paul healed a lame man, the crowd of Gentiles immediately began chanting that He and Barnabas were gods. This blasphemy frightened the apostles.

No, no, we are mere men.

Turn from foolish idols!

The true God is invisible, yet has displayed His generous goodness, and His love for you!

These pagans, who so worshipped them, were soon led otherwise by Jews from earlier cities of the tour. They stoned Paul until they thought he was dead.

The apostles went on to Derbe, and, in spite of the dangers slumbering in the cities they had left, retraced their steps back to Perga. At every point they strengthened their converts and set up pastors and congregational order.

From a port near Perga, Paul and his friend sailed directly to Antioch in Syria, concluding their mission.

In Antioch, the church was being told that only Jews could become Christians, therefore Greeks would have to become Jews before becoming Christians. Paul and Barnabas were sent to Jerusalem to settle the problem—which had come from die-hard Pharisees.

In church conference the question was argued. Peter's comments proved decisive.

Why would we vote against that which God has clearly done in opening His door to all?

After Barnabas and Paul recounted their experience, James, the president of the congregation (and brother of Jesus) declared against the Judaizers, and the church members voted in agreement. The Jerusalem apostles sent a letter, with authenticating witnesses, demanding only that Gentiles separate from paganism.

So, Paul and Barnabas, with the Jerusalem emmisaries, Judas and Silas, returned to Syrian Antioch to a rejoicing church. Silas decided to remain in Antioch.

When Paul announced a second missionary tour, he broke with beloved Barnabas over Mark. So, Mark went with Barnabas to his home on Cyprus, and Paul and Silas became a team.

In Lystra, young Timothy joined the team, and was circumcised as a matter of diplomacy (he was half Greek). The three then delivered the Jerusalem letter to the churches of Asia Minor.

They felt compelled, more and more, to push westward, until they found themselves at the sea, facing Europe. God called them over. Luke the physician there became the fourth member of the team, sailing over with them.

Their destination was Philippi, a very Roman city, with only a small Jewish community. Lydia, a businesswoman there, was born again, becoming the first European convert—and she won others.

A young medium harrassed the missionaries for several days until Paul totally destroyed her demonic spell. Her exploiters had Paul and Silas arrested, beaten, and imprisoned.

Prayer shook the jail at midnight. Paul's concern was for the frightened jailor, and he, and his family, were saved and baptized.

When the preachers revealed that they were Roman citizens, they were freed. To protect the officials from the Empire's discipline, they left Philippi.

In Thessalonica, there was a larger Jewish community, and three weeks of preaching produced many converts, both Jewish and Gentile. But resentful Jews, enlisting the help of thugs, caused trouble and blamed it on the believers. Paul and Silas had to slip out by night.

The Jews of Berea were open minded, and actually studied the Scriptures with Paul and Silas. But, when troublemakers arrived from Thessalonica, Paul was forced to flee to Athens.

Athens was a sophisticated pagan city (with a synagogue).

The Apostle was invited to speak to the

'thinkers,' and on Mars hill, he spoke of the nature of God and of man.

God is invisible, and to know Him revelation is required.

God's Temple is man's heart.

And all hearts are alike, in whatever time or place.

God is near to mankind; He cannot be brought nearer by statues.

All men must come to grips with Jesus Christ, Judgment, and resurrection of the dead.

Some Athenians were born again.

Silas and Timothy did not arrive at Athens, so Paul traveled alone to Corinth. After finding a job, he began preaching to Jews, but amid persecution, and sorrow, he turned to the Gentiles. When Silas and Timothy came through town, they found Paul preaching with sadness because the Jews so opposed him.

He finally proclaimed the synagogue to be heathen, and walked out, entering a Gentile's house in their full view. It developed that the president of the synagogue became a Christian.

After the Lord soothed Paul's fears, he remained in Corinth for eighteen months. The antiChristian feeling of the Jews grew stronger than ever, and in a united front they created so much trouble (though it somewhat turned on them) that the Apostle at last left.

Paul's fellow tent-maker, Acquilla, who had vowed not to cut his hair until Paul was safe, escorted the Apostle, and when they safely arrived at the port, he finally got his hair cut. He then, with his wife, sailed to Ephesus with Paul.

Paul, after a brief call on the Jewish synagogue in Ephesus, sailed on alone to Palestine. From Caesarea he visited the church in Jerusalem, and then sailed north to the home-base of Syrian Antioch.

A third missionary trip was in Paul's heart, and soon he was off again. He revisited his churches en route to Ephesus. Acquilla and his wife Priscilla were still in Ephesus. They had had opportunity to instruct in Christ a great Jewish biblical orator named Apollos. Apollos had already gone on to Corinth when Paul reached Ephesus.

At Ephesus, Paul met a few of John the Baptist's many disciples who had never personally heard the great prophet, and did not know of his instructions to believe on Jesus as Messiah and Saviour. But, on hearing from Paul, they accepted all.

After preaching for three months in the synagogue, Paul had to move to a schoolhouse, where he taught for the next two years. The city saw his great power to dispel human suffering.

In the failure of charlatans to use 'Jesus' commercially, there was a verification of the Heavenly source of the Apostle's power.

Paul began longing to see these great things occur in Rome herself.

But before Paul could leave Ephesus, the concern of pagan businessmen over the spreading of the Christian way of life erupted. Idol makers, worried about a fall-off in their trade, incited hysteria, and brought the entire city as a mob into the amphitheater. It was an explosive situation, with pagan antiChristian and antiJewish passions boiling. The mob was finally calmed by a city official who reminded them of their accountability to Rome.

Paul then left and revisited Europe. For several months he worked under the strain of a hunted man. Rome would have to wait.

He and his party returned to Asia, en route to Jerusalem—to fight the Jewish issue to a conclusion.

At the port city of Troas (in Turkey), Paul preached in the Sunday evening church service. During his extremely long sermon, a man fell three floors to his death. Paul restored the man's life, and then continued with the fellowship as if there would never be another chance.

The next day, desiring to take a long walk, Paul arranged to meet Luke and the ship at the next port, twenty miles away.

111

At the next layover, Miletus, Paul called for the Elders from Ephesus (fifty miles away), and bade them farewell.

In danger, I have faithfully served.

In danger, I move ahead.

In all, I have served the souls of all men and never have feared to preach the truth.

You must serve and guard God's church.

My life I leave as your example.

With a sense of finality, they knelt and prayed together.

Paul and Luke sailed on to Tyre, in Phoenicia. There the Apostle received urgent warnings about Jerusalem.

In Caesarea, at Philip the deacon-evangelist's home, so graphically did a Jerusalem prophet urge Paul to avoid the holy city that Luke also begged him to detour. Though heartbroken, Paul would not evade his sense of responsibility—the Jewish issue had to be faced in the most direct manner.

No sooner were Paul and his party in Jerusalem than the issue broke. Thousands of Jewish Christians had been led to believe that Paul was *inverting* the Council letter (which had freed Gentile believers from becoming Jews).

Many reports had arrived that Paul was actually teaching Jews to accept pagan-like freedom from Jewish law!

The Apostle to the Nations agreed to demonstrate his Jewish loyalty. But when he entered the Temple court to perform a ceremony, the blindly bigoted Jewish contingent from Asia Minor (Turkey) prejudicially assumed that he was there to somehow show contempt for their established customs. When these enemies inflamed the crowd of worshippers, the Roman soldiers (who surveyed all from a nearby tower) rescued him from the frenzied mob.

En route to the fortress, Paul was permitted to address the Jews. He spoke in the calming, sacred Hebrew tongue.

I, a life-long devoted Jew, once hated Jesus as you do.

But I saw Him in brilliant glory.

Yes, He stopped me on my journey of hate, and in the presence of Jewish witnesses.

I surrendered to His deity.

A devout Jew in Damascus received a revelation about me.

Later I saw Jesus in this very Temple— and here I received my commission to go to the Gentiles.

113

The audience erupted at this 'blasphemy.' Paul would have been scourged—but he was a Roman citizen of Tarsus. The Romans ordered the Jews to convene their own court.

The High Priest considered Paul's profession of loyalty a rank contempt of court. Paul responded by condemning the High Priest (who was actually merely an appointee of the Syrian governor). He divided the Council members in issues over which they had long fiercely disagreed among themselves. Again, the Romans, observing from their tower, rescued Paul from another murderous mob.

The Apostle was again held in custody. A massive Jewish murder plot was discovered by Paul's nephew, who then informed the Roman authorities. They moved Paul to the coastal city of Caesarea, which was the seat of Roman government for Judea-Samaria.

Felix (a successor of the first governor, Pontius Pilate—who heard the Jewish accusations against Christ) now heard the Jewish High Priest accuse Christ's Apostle. A clever prosecutor also spat vicious lies. Paul answered for himself.

> I was not in Jerusalem long enough to plot any conspiracies, and, as a matter of fact, no one saw or heard me do anything wrong.
>
> I am a loyal Jew, and respect all men.
>
> Those Asian Jews who charged me are

*not even here—obviously they have
nothing factual to say.*

Since there were no witnesses, Felix determined to hold Paul in house arrest until the
Roman captain could appear and describe the
Temple events. Felix showed some interest in
Paul's message, but could not allow himself, a
strong Roman, to think of profound spiritual
realities.

Two years later, when the new governor took
office, Paul was still a prisoner.

The new procurator, Festus, foiled a new
Jewish murder plot against Paul, and proceeded
to conduct another trial. When the evidence ex-
onerated Paul, Festus, to please the Jews, joined
the scheme to assassinate the prisoner. But Paul
interfered—he appealed to Caesar.

Herod Agrippa ruled for Rome, a district just
north of Galilee. He and his sister, Bernice, paid
a visit to Festus, and learned at length of Paul's
story. They were very interested. So, with great
ceremony the famous Jewish Christian, Paul,
was brought before the visitors. Festus hoped
through this to gain support in his decision to
send Paul to Rome. Paul preached to the
dignitaries.

*Many Jews know my background—I
have always been earnestly devoted to
true religion.*

My hope is the Jewish hope.

Yes, and once I was an antiChristian zealot.

But I saw Jesus in His brilliant Glory and heard His voice. I could not resist the facts.

Jesus sent me to all men. I have traveled everywhere preaching the good news—for this my enemies seek my life.

But all that I preach is in harmony with the Scriptures.

Festus hurled a personal slur, which Paul answered, and then Paul appealed to Agrippa— but the king had only an evasive reply.

Sailing with Paul to Rome was Luke the physician.

At Sidon, Phoenicia, the prisoner was allowed to visit friends.

After Sidon, the weather was bad, and steadily grew worse.

The ship struggled past Cyprus and anchored at a (Turkish) port, where the prisoners were transferred to an Egyptian vessel bound for Rome.

More bad weather prevented the ship from docking at its next port-of-call and forced it southward below the Island of Crete. While the ship rested at Fair Havens, Crete, the full force of a major winter storm began to be felt.

Paul warned the captain against sailing at that time, but a sudden break in the weather prompted him to sail on. No sooner had they struck anchor than the weather changed again, with such vengence that the crew lost all control. At one point the sailors girded the ship's hull with great ropes, actually tying it together—so frightened were they that they might be blown to Africa and be cast upon dangerous marshes which would tear the bark apart.

While all hands were working furiously throwing cargo overboard and otherwise trying to save the ship, an angel appeared to Paul and assured him of the safety of everyone. The storm had already lasted two weeks.

Respecting Paul's assurance, the Captain obeyed his advice to prevent anyone from abandoning ship. For the first time in days, all relaxed enough to eat.

Land was discovered. While trying to maneuver a landing, the bow of the ship stuck on a sandbar, and angry waves lashed the stern against rocks, breaking the ship up in spite of the rope binding. All two hundred and seventy six on board safely swam to shore. It was the Island of Malta.

Because Paul was unharmed when a poisonous snake struck him, the residents held him in awe. Paul healed the governor's father, and many others. The stranded party was hospitably treated.

Three months passed, and another Egyptian ship took them on to Italy. Believers from Rome met Paul and Luke about forty miles from the city to escort them into the capital of the world.

In Rome, Paul was permitted to choose his quarters. He found a place where he could exchange thoughts with the Jewish community. One long day was spent explaining to them the whole Gospel story. Before the Jews left that day, Paul made it clear that God was calling all nations, as equals with Israel.

God's *Empire Builder* thus preached the Gospel in Rome for two years. His desire, born during the Ephesus revival, and God's eternal plan, were fulfilled.

Romans

Dear Christians in Rome:

Jesus Christ is yesterday's promise and today's salvation.

I yearn to personally explain all this to you believers in order to strengthen your already famous faith in Christ. Of course, I would myself receive great spiritual benefits in the discharging of my sacred duty to the capital of the pagan world.

The Gospel is salvation for all; it supplies all God ever requires of any man. As they are, all men are lost without excuse, having abused the common blessings of life and having degenerated into twisted beings worshipping idols.

> Mankind's condemnation is just; the indictment is full: perversity in the body, filth in the mind, brutal selfishness in every relationship of life.

And there is sufficient cause to include even the best of men in this judgment; for they, also, often ignore basic truths while presuming on God's generous love. Yes, God is absolutely impartial in every respect, as 'good men's' secrets will someday prove. Many, many religious people work at being acceptable but miss these fundamental facts displaying the necessity of all men being born again.

Even a Bible-centered background, as valuable as such a heritage is, must not be permitted to obscure the reality that each man must be born again.

> God will count any man PERFECT if he will ADMIT his sin and ACCEPT God's gift of salvation, made possible by the blood of the Saviour covering his sins.

Salvation thus produces humility in the converts as it satisfies all of God's demands. No one has ever found God apart from this salvation by grace (God's generous love). The Bible sings and rings with the doctrine; it has always been true for all peoples of all times.

The ancient fathers of our Jewish Faith simply accepted God's promises (long before religious laws were written) and believed them. As soon as they believed, they were justified before Him, exactly as we are.

So, Salvation by Grace gives us peace in the presence of God.

For, if God's Son would die to save us,
He surely will keep us saved.

Adam's disobedience introduced sin, produc-ing death; but God's grace is greater and freely saves all who simply believe. Jesus Christ was obedient in life and in death, and His obedience is credited to each believer's account.

This will not allow moral carelessness because the born-again have 'buried' the old sin-ful thought patterns (as pictured in the 'burial' of baptism). The new birth (as pictured in the 'resurrection' of baptism) is always ac-companied by the death of the old desire to live in sin.

When you realize this has occured, you will have a wonderful assurance of salvation. You will still struggle with daily temptation and sin, but what you really are in your heart of hearts can have con-stant expression. Before being born again, you were in an endless circle of slavish sin and death. Now you are in an endless cir-cle of freely given salvation and vic-torious life.

No citizen is exempt from the law; but there are no laws binding *dead* men. (Death even removes the laws of marriage.) In such a way, each believer is the same as dead when it comes to being forced to observe religious rules and ceremonies. He is simply a man free to do what Christ has placed in his heart.

121

In no way is this to 'throw-off' on the Ten Commandments; they convince lost men of their sins and they remind the believer of the profound weaknesses and sin still present in his old nature. So, while his innermost being is alive with passion to please Jesus Christ, his outward being must continually remember and obey God's laws of duty and morality.

The believer's assurance of salvation springs not from his keeping of the Commandments, but from the fact of the new birth: he knows he has a new mind from the Spirit of God. This is also the power to cause his weak body to actually walk the paths of righteousness. The whole Christian life is *freedom* and *assurance.*

Yes, the Father hears the Christian's cries and the Spirit whispers assurance of ultimate total victory for him and for all of creation at the resurrection. But heartache will not disappear before that day. Until then, the Holy Spirit comforts and helps, and God's Word guarantees eternal victory.

So, the Gospel of Christ answers every urgent question of life and implants perfect peace.

I love Israel, but no nation or religion can save anyone; only God's grace can do that. And Israel's very birth was a matter of God's grace, regardless of what anyone might say. All of her blessings and persecutions have been God's doings, without man's advice. He has permitted the heathen, though totally ungodly, to flourish so that they might be born again and share in the church with born-again Jews.

One Prophet said:

I will embrace and love the ungodly.
The heathen shall be My people.

Another prophet said:

Only a few Jews will ever be saved;
God would have to wait forever for more
to humble themselves to be born again.

And:

Only by His mercy are any Israelites
saved.

The ignorant nations, by God's grace, have found the knowledge of salvation, but the priviledged People have missed it because they were intent upon trusting their own good works. I pray and pray for Israel; if only their genius could be combined with knowledge. But they live in the past, and their questions are, too often, argumentative evasions and not honest inquiries. They should know that the only thing necessary to do God's will is a simple 'yes.' The Lord Jesus Christ is now giving eternal life in honor of that humble response. Yes, 'faith only' opens the door to all; anyone who wants to be saved, can—simply by accepting Christ.

And God desires this 'yes' from all. But no one can so 'call' on the Lord or 'believe' in the

Lord unless he accepts the basic facts of the Gospel as delivered by one of God's messengers.

No, neither heathen nor Jew can be saved until someone who knows the truth goes to him and presents the message. However, the preacher cannot expect everyone who hears to believe, even though the preaching of the Word has the power to create faith. Israel has heard God's Word, even concerning His mercy to the heathen. But hearing is not all; the hearer has a soverign will, which he must surrender.

God still loves Jews. And still there are many Jews who love God; they have accepted the way of faith without works. But most Jews are lost; their spiritual condition is very, very sad indeed. However, their plight has opened the way for the heathen to find God. And whenever Jews themselves find God's personal salvation the nations will reap even greater spiritual benefits.

I do hope these words stimulate many fellow Jews to seek and find God's truth. What a wonderful day it will be. Jews will forever, because of their heritage, have a unique opportunity to bless mankind whenever they accept the Gospel; Gentiles might as well admit this is true, and know also that any Gospel-blessed nation can lose its blessings through apostasy.

Please learn these lessons of spiritual history:

(1) true blessings cannot be inherited; (2) any generation can lose what the former had received; and, (3) once lost, the blessings can be restored—by God's grace.

This will happen to Israel. Although they are now enemies of God, He still does, and forever will, love them in a special way. Their chastening has brought the Gospel to the nations. Now, the very fact that God's mercy is offered to degenerate, sinful, heathen pagans is itself a wide-open door for the disobedient Jews.

Only the infinite attributes of the eternal God of love could so arrange to shower benefits upon enemies and redeem the castaways of the world— while never forsaking equity and justice!

No one could have anticipated this.

No man would ever have initiated this.

God conceives, controls, and consummates.

Dedication to the Lord is a very personal matter; it begins with a realistic self-evaluation and a willingness to serve appropriately in a congregation. It involves rejecting evil and displaying love in every situation and relationship of life. It demands a resolve to live in peace, leaving all retaliations to God.

The committed Christian is a good citizen, respectfully paying taxes and his bills, yet with

125

such a big debt of love to mankind that he can never pay it in full. Love makes a good citizen and a good neighbor. Someone must give love and holy dedication in this world—and it is we who know the Lord.

The congregation must be filled with charity; members should never criticize one another's personal opinions. Just assume that each is doing the best he can, and that he is the property and responsibility of Christ. Spend all your thought on serving the brother you feel is weak, then you, yourself, will be above criticism. Maturity and dedication to congregational peace will be accompanied by great personal tranquility.

Congregational unity rests upon the strong who bear with the weak; such is the prescription for church health. People of all backgrounds and conditions should find a generous welcome in the assembly. I think you understand.

I don't hesitate to state this revolutionary idea of spiritual democracy. I know it is God's will. It is part of the powerful Good News I preach everywhere.

Because I have given myself to pioneer work, I have not yet visited Rome with its already existing church. But later, I do hope to come. Now I go to take financial help to the believers in Jerusalem (here is an example of Gentile helping Jew), then I will see you. However, there are grave difficulties which God must overcome to bring me to Rome.

Phoebe, a Corinthian businesswoman, is delivering this letter to you. Priscilla and Aquilla, my dear protectors when I lived in danger of death in Corinth, are now in Rome. So many of my converts and co-workers (and relatives) are also now in Rome. I remember and love them all so much—I wish I could kiss each one.

I deeply resent those heretics who would split congregations by pretending to tell people sophisticated secrets. I pray you will be content as 'simple' believers—the Gospel is *our* secret and power.

Timothy and others are with me, and think of you. The entire Corinthian church greets you.

I commit you to God. He is the Author of this Gospel, which accepts all men just as they are, and, through the new birth, places them on an equal level before Him—and in the congregation.

Paul

1 Corinthians

Dear Corinthians,

May this letter speak to you and everyone everywhere who has answered God's call to the pure and clean life of a believer in Jesus Christ.

Your congregation is especially blessed with a very broad range of talents, and God alone is to be praised for this. But, sad to say, you are praising men and thus dividing the church. Personally, I reject that kind of praise; I am simply a messenger. And my message actually debases human wisdom, being so far above any man's highest thought. It has built your congregation out of slaves, burned-out castaways, and unlettered nobodies, and deposited in your very beings the treasures of time and eternity. Only the Christ of this message deserves to be praised.

So powerful is the Gospel that it requires no great human talent to make it work, and it certainly did not originate *from* human talent—the Holy Spirit of God dictated every word. I simply yielded to the Holy Spirit in order to become a messenger.

Now, you must yield to the Spirit in order to grow spiritually. At present, your minds are fixed upon human relationships. These leaders you 'worship' are incidental to God's purpose— which is *you,* yourselves. All leaders will be judged according to the contribution they make to you. The *congregation* is the Temple of God. Any preacher who builds himself destroys himself. The *congregation* must be built, honored, embellished and protected.

This is exactly what I do. God knows it is true; He knows my very heart. Now you must grow up! Stop playing games; Christianity is serious business. Living for Christ has cost me everything. Now honor me by following me in service. Timothy will instruct you further in how to serve. I hope things improve before I come.

You must resolve the question of immorality in the church. It cannot be tolerated. You have a wrong-headed broad-mindedness. There is no room in Christ's blood-bought congregation for permissiveness toward immorality. While it is necessary to deal with immoral unsaved people, to treat an immoral person as a Christian brother is absolutely forbidden.

And then you treat fellow Christians as heathen by suing them in pagan courts. You must settle your own differences. Any humble believer can act as arbiter between church members. When one insists on vindication he is self-evidently in error.

130

Impurity forbids the presence of God. Christ erases the past and gives liberty. Although our bodies will decay, they are sacred. To misuse them in immorality is unthinkable. Body and spirit together form the Temple of the Holy Spirit—a reality made possible by the Cross.

In answer to your inquiries:

No, it is no sin to be unmarried, although marriage is the normal course for all. All married partners must defer to one another: neither husband nor wife is sole ruler of his or her own body. There is reciprocal ownership and one must always be available to the other.

While marriage is a matter of free choice (in dangerous times there is distinct advantage in being single), God gives no freedom to destroy an existing marriage—even if one partner is unsaved. Even a mixed marriage is legal and sacred, and binding in every respect—until the unsaved mate walks out.

You cannot redo the past. Just daily do God's will. Don't worry about where you now find yourself in life—right there is where God wants to use you.

Back to the question of the unmarried: at present their condition is to be preferred, but certainly not demanded. Whatever you do, keep eternity's values in view. The unmarried can give themselves more to pioneer Christian work and therein receive great blessings. Now I know that a couple in love differ from those making theoretical decisions.

A widow is, of course, an unmarried person, and usually she will do better to remain a widow—though she is perfectly free to re-marry.

Many religious taboos are meaningless. But, even though idols and images are *nothings,* many former pagans still consider them to have real evil power. Therefore, it may be wise for me to observe some overscrupulous restrictions.

To my detractors, I defend my office. (But to you, my converts, no defense is necessary.) I have full right to accept a salary, even support for a family if I had one. I am thoroughly aware of the basis for this right of remuneration— including the clear commands of Christ. But I have foregone all these normal advantages.

I *must* preach the Gospel. And it must never even be hinted that I preached it for any other reason than that *I wanted to* with all my heart and soul.

Love is my motive; humble service is my method. I am anybody's slave. I am reaching for a crown worth any sacrifice and discomfort.

You, yourselves, can win an eternal prize. You can forsake materialism, adultery, discontent, and arrogance, with God's help.

Paganism has nothing for thoughtful men;

the church offers fellowship with God. Christian participation in heathen worship is unthinkable to the point of absolute absurdity.

But there is no need to trace the religious history of cut-rate food, or to question the host at a meal. If someone raises a question, then it is proper to yield to his scruples, however ill-advised. God is honored when you respect any man's convictions on nonessential matters. This is the way I personally live.

But no man is to surrender totally to anyone. (The wife, of course, must, in a sense, so surrender.) Since, there in Greece, it is customary for inferiors to show their position by wearing head-coverings, wives should be careful to wear the veil. (In no way are we thus accepting the degrading Greek concept of womanhood.) Wearing a veil is consistent with Christian propriety and universal human instinct. Christians should never argue with acceptable cultural customs. It would be better to close the church than to have a divided congregation which uses the communion service to build cliques. The Sacred Supper is the Lord's. He died to make it possible and its abuse is a serious matter. Yes, congregational harmony is essential at the Lord's Table.

Understand how the Spirit works. He is no speechless statue; He speaks through men who honor Jesus. And men honor Jesus through their individual abilities. Yes, the Holy Spirit speaks and moves through many consecrated people to build up the congregation, which, in a sense, is Christ in this world.

So, the congregation should function as one divine Person. Thus, everyone has a royal position; everyone is essential. However, there are priorities and subordinations which demand recognition and thought.

The most wonderful expression of the Holy Spirit is *Love,* without which He never speaks through anyone.

Love is perfect for all human relationships of this life and will never lead to embarrassment in Eternity when we finally learn how little we have known about so many things.

Love speaks louder than anything.

So, in love, seek to be used of the Spirit by spreading true knowledge. To do so, one must speak in plain language with a desire to help others. Why talk to one's self? Helping others is the purpose of the Spirit. So plain talk is a necessary tool. Every language is *good,* but any language is *insulting* when the listener does not know it. The Holy Spirit wants to speak through you, but you must be understood in order to convey His message. You who speak foreign tongues should seek the ability to speak in the local language. (Even when I pray I want to teach people.) Let the Spirit pray and sing through you in the local language and you will be a builder of men.

I know and use many languages, but to show them off in church would be childish.

Isaiah said:

> *When God speaks in foreign languages through conquering soldiers, it is evidence of His utter rejection.*

Surely that is not the work you want. But, more than that, the unsaved will think you are crazy when you speak in a language they can't understand.

A Gospel meeting should be an overpoweringly convincing experience for lost men. It always is when every believer contributes in an orderly and meaningful manner. Don't blame confusion on the Holy Spirit's inspiration. (Both common intuition and Scripture dictate that women are not to be ministers in the church.)

Now decide if you are going to *give* God's truth—and not *receive* it only. No one is an organ of the Holy Spirit without a burning ambition to win the lost and build the brethren. If this does not settle any man's confusion over 'tongues,' nothing will.

Here is the message to make clear to all:

Christ fulfilled the Scriptures when He died and arose from the dead. And He did all this as our substitute. And there is absolute proof that He is alive.

He came to me and made me an authoritative pioneer missionary to plant churches over the world. I have let no one out-do me. The resurrection of Jesus is the power that saved your souls.

Oh yes, there is resurrection from the grave. Christianity, with all our hopes, is founded on that fact.

Christ arose. We shall rise. One day *death* shall die. One day the mission of Christ will be complete. (Baptism pictures the victory of resur-rection.) Because I believe in resurrection, I ex-pose myself to danger every hour of every day in every way. Christian service cannot exist apart from this creed.

Anyone should know that decay does not prevent resurrection and that the new body is greater than the seed from whose decomposi-tion it springs. The original body is a kind of seed of the future one which shall be entirely different. The new body will have the strength to obey our heart's purest desire. We now bear the weight of sinful bodies but then there shall be no such burden. Our new bodies will not in-terfere with the enjoyment of the presence of God.

We'll be new, instantly, whether decom-posed or breathing. We will have won. We will sing and shout the victory. So, we'll work till Jesus comes.

The believers in famine-stricken Jerusalem

are depending upon you and other churches. So each week, lay aside as you can, funds for their relief. When I arrive you should have enough to send by messengers (I might go myself) to the holy city. As for now, I intend to stay with you several months after I leave Ephesus with its great opportunities and dangers.

Should Timothy arrive, remember that he deserves full honor.

Apollos refused my urgings to visit you at this time.

Be brave men. Serve with love. Note the mature Christians and listen to them.

Those traveling 'helpers,' Stephanas, Fortunatus, and Achaicus have arrived. They are helping in your name. You know how much men like these mean to Gospel work.

Everyone here sends you greetings. Each one of you, please go to a brother and kiss him for us.

I add this to my secretary's manuscript:

'It is love for Jesus that counts!'

'I want to see that resurrection day.'

'God bless you. I love you.'

In Jesus name,

Paul

2 Corinthians

Dear Corinthian congregation,

There is abundant peace for you, who, through Jesus Christ, know God as your Father. I have experienced His comfort; it is always equal to my pain. So I know that God will watch over you.

In Asia (Turkey) I was a 'dead man,' but God kept on rescuing me, and will, as long as so many of you keep on praying for me.

I know I am honestly doing God's will, and you have nothing to be ashamed of in me. The fact that my travel plans change displays no deceit at all. No, just as I preach a dependable Gospel message, I always speak plainly.

It was just to spare you my anger that I cancelled my visit. I don't want to be your dictator, so I left you to the Holy Spirit.

I want to count on *freely* exchanged love and support. With streaming tears I wrote my other letter, not to sadden you, but hoping to convey my love.

You evidently were saddened, as I, in that certain member's awful sin (which you had *seemed* to tolerate.) Your freely taken vote to expel him saved him (now forgive and forget) and proved that the new birth works in pagan hearts. I forgive that man also. We have wrestled with Satan himself in this issue.

I left Ephesus for Troas to learn of your vote; I confess, I was very anxious. But, Halleleujah! There is victory on every side. My ministry has been vindicated in the reality of your born-again hearts. Oh, I didn't do it, the *Gospel* did it—not *law* and *coercion.*

The Gospel does work in pagan hearts and a new day has dawned for mankind! No preacher need use any threat or device to obtain obedience. (Coercion actually hides God.) Now the whole world can see that the new birth produces hearts, even in pagans, that voluntarily desire to obey righteousness.

I will never stop preaching this as plainly as I possibly can. Only a veil from Satan could hide this Gospel light—which makes my heart seem like a great light-house; and yet I feel so acutely the utter weakness of my being. Sometimes I think I will break under the strain, but God holds me together; so often I don't know what to do, but God gives just enough daily direction. When it seems all are against me, I am reminded that somewhere there are those who love God, and me. I get a lot of knock-downs, but, thank God, have never been knocked out. But then, things have not changed much since Jesus had to *die* to give freedom to men.

I, too, do all this for you. Like Jesus, I believe God's Word, so I know that I'll be with you in the resurrection. Your congregation is what it's all about.

So, I never stop. My dying body houses a soul of eternal youth. I wear this veil of clay for an instant only, but will shine with brilliance forever and ever. That light in my heart is eternal; the passing scene fades.

Yes, when my frail tent here is folded I will be robed in immortality. (This was God's purpose for us when He made us, and is guaranteed the moment we are born again.) Such a faith produces confidence in the face of death.

I don't want to be ashamed of my service when I see Him—so I open myself to you as God knows me. You need this clear picture of sincerity and love. I count my life to have already ended; this is a 'second existence' in which I just abandon myself to Christ. Everything I desired for so many years is forgotten. This is what it means to be 'born again.' Now my thoughts are of Jesus Christ, the Saviour of the world, and of myself as His royal ambassador begging men to accept the peace He has made through His Cross. So I have entreated you with all urgency.

And in honor of that high office and mission I suffer anguish, and pain, often working night and day without food. I guard my heart and attitudes and yield to the Holy Spirit. I leave no battle of faith unfought. So I know in my heart that many opinions of me are petty and ill-conceived. But in my anguish and poverty I have shown you joy and given you riches untold.

No honest man can stumble over any part of my ministry. Surely no one will stumble over my life: I am in constant need and perpetual trouble, yet display sincerity and power. I promote and defend the Gospel, I accept unkind judgments, ignominy, and ridicule—just leaving all in God's hands.

In not one thing has my ministry been a cause of stumbling. I have suffered mental anguish, and bodily abuse, yet I have displayed sincerity, insight, self control, generous love, and miraculous power. Since I have defended the Faith as well as evangelized, I have gained totally opposite evaluations. With my nothing I have enriched many.

Now you can see how I love you—and the concern I have when your affections seem frozen.

Please don't be alienated by any compromise with pagan religion: your church must never make common cause with those who reject the Faith. Your congregation must shine in

Corinth as the Temple where God actually lives in His children. What an opportunity for purity of life and worship!

I am totally yours. My heart beats for you, and now you have thrilled me beyond words. You have lifted me from despair by your vote which represented true, uncoerced repentance. (Titus met me and reported all.) My other letter was successful. Titus saw it. I was vindicated; you were proved. The Gospel works.

The churches of northern Greece (Macedonia), even in penury, have given much to the destitute of Jerusalem. Now that your church has passed this crucial test (proving yourselves born-again) you can imitate Christian sacrificial giving.

Just do what you can. Right now you have more than the Jerusalem believers—but the situation could reverse itself. Titus (with this letter) and another brother will return to Corinth; having two or three signatures protects integrity in money handling.

This reminder is hardly necessary, but I have boasted so much of you that I cannot risk anyone's embarrassment. Now let loving generosity flow; God will generously take care of you. I pray He will bless your plantings and your harvests. I know this offering is being blessed not only in feeding hungry people but in demonstrating that the poorest of lost pagans, when born again, become generous Christians.

143

Hallelujah! This is what God has now given the world.

When I was in Corinth, I never did browbeat you. Now, I beg you. I have waited to do more, for good reason. I have carefully restrained and limited my expression of authority. My only desire is to do my work so well that I can have permission to press on to unsown fields in distant lands. And this permission is entirely in God's hand.

Wait! I'm no fool! I am just a *father* worried about his daughter. Isn't that enough to cause one to be careful in the exercise of power?

Did I hurt you by not getting your money? No! The way I work humiliates only those imposter preachers who would enslave you. No, I'm no fool. But, since it seems your only 'wise men' are those who treat you as dirt, maybe I am.

If *I'm* a fool, *they* must be *second-class fools;* for I am all the things they brag about, plus I have a great catalogue of sufferings and exploits for Jesus Christ. I love all the churches and suffer with each and every member. Like a fool, I am proud of these my *weaknesses.*

But I go further: I have taught from a great untapped reserve of divine knowledge. To brag of this would make me an out-and-out fool. Receiving this knowledge left in me a perpetual agony; but through that pain I have learned to lean on Jesus for everything. So, still, my weakness is my boast! But, instead of hearing me boast, you should be thanking me for bringing the power of the Holy Spirit to your town—without charge.

I'm returning to you; again, I will give and not receive.

I speak not these things for my own benefit. I want to make you strong; and I am afraid of coming with these things unsettled in your minds. I don't want to be proven wrong in my bright expectations of you. Each visit is a witness of the truth. You have had long enough (two visits) to accept my credentials. So this time, I will treat all who still reject me as hopelessly lost.

So check yourselves out. I want you right for your own sakes, so I won't have to oppose you. When you are right with God I appear to be very weak because that is the point—your strength—and it has been acheived.

Good-bye; leave nothing undone, live harmoniously. Remember the kiss of love. The other churches think of you.

Paul

145

Galations

Dear believers of central Asia-Minor,

You are no longer slaves of circumstances; God be praised.

That you are wavering is unbelievable. How could you see anyone who confuses the Gospel as less than a devil?—I care not how you take that. I'm no part of any *machine*. I used to be, but the God of my salvation chose that I never again be in any such relationship, however good in itself it may be. That is not to say that the established Christian leaders have not, from the first, fully recognized me.

And when God led me, just recently, to visit the leaders in Jerusalem it was to protect my churches from destructive dangers of *machine-minded boys* from the mother church confusing us and ruining them. I was totally successful. (The whole thing came about because of imposters with seemingly valid credentials from Jerusalem trying to enslave the Antioch, Syrian church.) Yes, the Jerusalem Apostles fully accepted me and bade me God-speed.

Even more recently, I have publicly corrected Peter, number two man in Jerusalem, when he seemed to endorse compromise with enslaving error.

You can't compromise truth without being two-faced.

To be saved out of a religious system of cultish group-pressure and then to actually send others into it is unthinkable.

There is a new group—neither Jew nor Gentile.

We are obviously evil if we attack something as wrong, and then support it.

I consider myself as having died and now enjoying a second existence, which is simply Jesus using my body. Only utter confusion could result from mixing the two lives—before and after being born again.

To you I preached Jesus and a new life in the new group, which has no human dictators. And now would you join an old group with hierarchial slavery?

The great Abraham was the picture of independence and nothing since him has improved the way of salvation. Keeping the Law of Moses has never even *helped* to save. It in no manner added to the plan of salvation, which has always been and always will be *faith alone.*

The Law of Moses filled a passing need in human relationships—it never pretended to offer new life. Indeed, the Scriptures declare all men to be Law-breakers and lost—with no hope but faith. There is no need for ceremonial and legalistic religious systems now that the Gospel is here with the Holy Spirit writing *obedience* on the heart of the born-again. This is all portrayed in baptism, which brings us into the fellowship of the new *free* group—Christians.

We are the full-grown product of history: no longer children being told what to do. Christ has come and given the inheritance due at maturity.

How foolish of you to now join a group which refuses its fortune as if still children under age of inheritance. Someone seems to be destroying all I have built. I forsook my *childhood* and became a man in Christ and now you want to live as I did when a child!

You have always been so kind to me. You accepted me with my illness which, originally, caused me to be in your country. And now you have been led to think I am holding you back from a deeper life with Christ which is supposedly entered by circumcised Jews only. No! You are regressing to childhood and infancy.

You desire now to be under Moses, but you are not listening to Moses tell about the two covenants: the Old with the enslaving rules and regulations, and the New with the Holy Spirit writing God's love on the heart. Moses teaches

149

that the two cannot be mixed.

Therefore stand! Accept a ritual, slavish approach to the spiritual life and you will become a slave living on the low plane of poverty. The only hope of a deeper life is through the Spirit working in our hearts. And faith's work is *love*.

Someone has thrown a rock in your path and added a little poison to your bread. But I think you will recover yourselves. How silly of my enemies to say to you that I preach what they preach. No, the Cross is the offending rock in their path.

Let these disturbers who would operate on men do even more to themselves!

Our liberty is the liberty to love, not the right to ignore our brother. So just follow the new Spirit in your hearts and you won't need laws to control your lusts. The Holy Spirit in your heart gives you victory over dark passions and produces beautiful graces needing no controls. Please devote all your thoughts to this wonderful Gospel life. Help your discouraged brother, don't condemn him. If you pay attention to your life you'll be aware of your own shortcomings.

Contribute to the support of your faithful teachers; you can't escape this responsibility. If you don't help the Gospel financially you will not mature spiritually. Do what's right because it is right and someday, somehow, you will see the good results.

Now let me add with my own impaired vision:

Spiritual dwarfs are trying to enslave you; they live in fear of some 'leader' somewhere.

But I died to all that when I learned the Gospel. Remember, the Spirit in your heart is what is real.

I have been scarred all over by violent persecution and this is my 'circumcision', showing my bondage to Christ.

Paul

Ephesians

Dear Christian congregations,

I write as a special messenger of Jesus Christ. I now enjoy the spiritual fulfillment which God has long planned for everyone who forsakes ceremonial religion and simply trusts in Jesus, who is the very expression of the Father's generous love. God informed me of His predetermined intention to culminate all spiritual history in the person and work of Jesus, thereby giving all who accept Him the fulfillment of children who have become men with rights to an inheritance.

Yes, Jews and Gentiles alike are born again by the Spirit of God, and this is just the first stage of the delivery of this great inheritance.

I pray that you new Christians will understand the mighty position with Christ which your congregations occupy.

Yes, you pagan Gentiles, and we religious Jews are born anew as trophies of God's generous love. Only Jews (and proselytes) were members of the Old congregations, but now,

153

simply by the new birth, Gentiles and Jews are together in the New congregations. Jesus, in His death, solved all separating problems. Both are now, together, the Temple of the Living God.

This is exactly why I am now under arrest; I want all Gentiles to know they can come directly to God without becoming Jews—and many Jews don't like the idea.

But God Himself gave me the ministry to unfold to the world this secret, long-kept in the heart of the Almighty. Now, through the existence of *Christian* congregations both political and spiritual dictators can see what God really thinks about the sovereignty of the individual soul. The fact that I am a prisoner just underscores the resistance which authorities exert toward the idea of *free men.*

I am overwhelmed with the immense significance of all this. I pray you will all grasp more and more of the profound scope of your spiritual position. Results beyond our thoughts will arise from these beginnings in which we now participate.

So, please, live the honor given you by loving all your fellow church members. You can't divide up the congregation; differences must be accepted and all abilities must be used to build one another. Then your fellowship will be stable and mature. Remember, you were once benighted pagans, but you have been born again, so you must cultivate generosity toward one another. Especially must your speech be full only of purity, love, and kindness.

Remember how God loved and saved you from the sewers of filth, and ordered you not to return. Christ raised you from spiritual death and made you to be lights to illumine the path of purity. So live with urgency and sobriety the Spirit-filled life of submission to one another.

Wives should honor their husbands, and especially must husbands surrender themselves to the needs of their wives—just as Jesus subordinated Himself to our needs. The man's sacrifice must be a total one.

It is the Lord's will for children to obey their parents and His command is set in a great promise of successful living, but parents are not at all to misuse their superior position.

If the employee (even slave), with a right attitude obeys the boss, however difficult it may be, he can expect to be blessed of the Lord. And the boss must not browbeat or mistreat the worker in any way. God sees no difference in them.

Ours is, in fact, a war against oppressive authorities, but our defense is purely spiritual. Nothing can defeat Truth, Peace, Faith, Salvation, and the Bible.

Pray, and pray for me that I will never flinch in the fight.

Tychicus delivers this letter from Rome and brings with him all the news of my work here.

Peace, Love, Faith, Grace.

Paul

Philippians

Dear Philippian Christians,

Timothy is with me here in Rome, and He joins me in greeting the pastors, deacons, and members of your church.

I have great gratitude for your support and every confidence that it will continue till Jesus comes. I've no timidity in this for I love you so much and have given you all that I have and am. And I have no deeper desire than that you may experience all the blessings of Christ.

Please know that, though under arrest, everyone in Rome knows I am no criminal, but simply a man of God in God's mighty hand. This has encouraged all believers. Oh, I know that some gospel preachers are actually increasing their work in a deliberately injurious manner, simply to cause my captors to think ill of me, and to alienate Christians from my support. But, by no means is this true of all or most fellow preachers. Truly, I am pleased, in spite of their unwise methods, to know that the Gospel is being spread.

And somehow, I know, everything together will result in the answer to my prayers. The desire of my heart, above all, is to be sincere, true, and courageous for Christ. This I desire above freedom, or even life. My purpose is not to live, but, to do God's will, and, at this time, it is His will, I am assured, to be freed, to live, and to see you again.

Now, guard your personal testimonies, your congregational unity, and the Christian Creed. Anyone opposing people who so live is evidently a child of Satan.

There is one way Christians can cheer up one another: by showing humble, sincere, unselfish brotherly love. That's the only way Christ ever thought—and look how the Father honors Him. Please, each of you, pay attention to these attributers in your own lives, you will then find God is at work in you. You won't, through arguing and complaining, be dimming your lamps.

When *you* shine with the Gospel I know *my* life is not wasted, even should I die now. (Of course this works both ways.)

When Timothy reaches you, please send him back with the encouraging report desired above. You can be sure, he loves you unselfishly.

Right now, I am returning Epaphroditus, recovered from a critical illness. You cannot but be encouraged when you see, or even hear about, someone who loves you as much as he. Think of what I have said and be encouraged with joy.

I cannot speak too strongly against those who add laws and rituals as necessary for salvation. Having a born-again heart is the only thing we need—and we have that!

Long ago I touched every base in the religious game, but God called me 'out.' When I lost all confidence in my good works to save me, I 'won.' Christ's goodness was counted as mine; I found Him as my personal Saviour; I was, as it were, raised from the dead.

And He has much, much more for me. With all my all, I want it all. More than anything, I want to live a life just as Jesus lived.

Mature Christians can pray for more wisdom. All should *do* what they already *know*. All can use my life as an example, a test. Doing so you will see how false teachers serve twisted emotions. Unlike them, we think of the spiritual world and long for the physical to be subservient to the Spirit.

So resist false doctrine and bad attitudes. In the simple Christian life there is joy, joy, joy. Sing the joy of Jesus and show it in your generosity, freedom from worry, and daily supply of peace. Cultivate pure and positive thinking.

I certainly appreciate your recent financial support. You know I am contentedly employed by Christ, and in every financial condition His power is seen in my life. You did His will in helping me and I am glad.

And I cannot forget the way you helped me in my missionary travels—you will reap in the harvest I have sown, for you helped. Your generosity proves your love is real, and He will prove Himself to you from the treasures of Heaven.

Let no one there miss my personal greetings. My little church of Caesar's slaves send their 'Hello.'

Paul

Colossians

To the congregation at Colossae,

Praise God! You are filled with Faith, Love, and Hope—Gospel preaching never fails; Epaphras truly preached the word. Now, never let up in the progress of your Christian life. Don't miss any of the birthright of *born-again dead men*.

Jesus the Lamb is God's only eternal Son, Brother to born-again sinner-sons because He arose from the dead to give lost men their new birth. He alone rules the congregations of His 'brethren'; they have no other God but Jesus the slain Lamb.

By paying the price of sin, Jesus introduced harmony into the universe. The vilest offenders are safe forever, the moment they truly believe on Jesus as their only hope. Providing that good news cost the blood of Jesus, and preaching it involves suffering and sacrifice, too. But how marvelous is the message—any man, regardless of his human heritage, is assured of Heaven and eternal joy when he turns to Jesus Christ. That's the truth the Christian messenger has to deliver.

God is known only through Jesus Christ, not through intricate systems of philosophy, nor any other supposed form of deity.

The newborn heart is the birthmark God gives. Baptism pictures it all: immersed—the man dead in sins and ignorance is buried; raised out of the water—he has been given a new life, because Jesus really paid the death penalty and arose from the grave. So, taboos, rituals—everything reminding a man of guilt—are destroyed forever. Real things have replaced object lessons.

So, there is no need to think of old doctrines of the spirit world, or to submit to the rules associated with the old thoughts.

We are so free, free to anticipate Heaven and eternal joy, free to combat the real evils of life, free to promote true godliness and spiritual unity befitting God's congregations and civilizations examples. To the entire world we have an immense responsibility requiring constant readiness.

Tychicus and Onesimus delivering this letter will bring personal news. My fellow prisoners here in Rome send their salute.

Epaphras never stops thinking of you and the other congregations in your part of Turkey.

My physician and fellow laborer, Luke, sends greetings.

You and the Ephesian congregation should swap letters so both can be read in the services of both churches.

Don't forget to let your present pastor know that you are fully behind him when he preaches the whole counsel of God.

I sign with love,

Paul

Don't forget to pray about my imprisonment. God bless you.

1 Thessalonians

Dear believers at Thessalonica,

Silas and Timothy have been traveling with me on this second missionary tour and they are with me here in Corinth after my refuge in Athens. To each of us it is a thrill to remember our wonderful experiences with you—notwithstanding the dangers, always so real.

Your conversions from paganism were so great—so magnificent! You carefully watched our lives as Christian missionaries and desired to know our joy—even if it meant sharing our persecutions. Now, you are the examples for your whole country. Everywhere I go, people have heard of your church and are constantly talking about your clear-cut conversions from your old idol worship and hopelessness.

And I know you haven't forgotten those days; how we arrived as refugees from Philippi, yet boldly preaching, even though the same troubles still hounded us. You immediately recognized our transparent sincerity. As a loving mother works night and day, so we found employment at night (as tentmakers) and preached during the day. And you will recall how, after the church was established, our instructions to you were not commands of dictators, but the expressions of a father's noblest paternal ambitions. Oh, shall I never forget how you accepted our sermons as the very Word of God! That's exactly how you came to faith in Christ. And like the Jews persecuted the churches of Palestine, so your fellow citizens have bitterly harrassed you. (What shame that my Jewish kinsmen would hate Jesus to the death and thus become the enemies of mankind, and how sad that this attitude is bringing the increasing wrath of Rome against their nation.)

The troubles that separated us have left me longing to come back to you. You are God's showpiece.

My heart so burned that, though I needed Timothy, I sent him from Athens to visit you. I was worried about all the persecutions you were experiencing. When he returned and met me here in Corinth, bearing your message of love, it made me feel that even should these troubles here in Corinth take my life, that I would continue to live on earth through you. I can't thank God enough for you—I just want to see you and give you my all.

Lord Jesus, please send me back to these dear people!

Let me again instruct you. We must establish

the institution of Christian marriage wherein people wed for love and not for selfish lust, and wherein partners stay married and do not seduce one another's mates. I know customs have been so lax in this area (because womanhood has been so disrespected) that some may think this harsh, but believe me, God places great priority on the sanctity of the home.

Your love of fellow Christians is well known, and I just say, keep on keeping on.

I'm sorry you have not understood about what happens when a Christian dies. We know that Jesus arose from death and will return someday and raise the bodies of our Christian loved ones. So, you see, the living have no advantage over the dead; bodies living and dead will be changed as we, together, meet the Lord at His coming.

Nothing can be said as to *when* He is coming. It would be ridiculous for God to tell anyone; the wicked don't deserve to know, and Christians don't need to know. They know Jesus Himself, serve Him, and are saved and secured by Him—this is perfect peace.

Remember to respect your pastors and superiors, esteem your equals, and encourage your inferiors. Do nothing but generous-minded good, even to mean-minded people.

Cultivate a happy attitude.

167

Be a peaceful, thankful people.

The Holy Spirit speaks through all Christians, so listen to everyone and weigh carefully what each says.

In questionable situations, give purity the benefit of every doubt.

I pray God your emotions, your body, your mind be pure and clean to the end. He gave you new hearts, and He will do this too.

I need your prayers.

Your brother needs your love.

Read this letter, as the Word of God, in your church services.

God bless you.

Paul

2 Thessalonians

Beloved church:

Silas and Timothy join my salute to you in the love of God.

You are so willing to believe the Lord, and to love one another; I am continuously using you as my sermon illustration. God must, because He is just, reward you for your sufferings for Him, and condemn to Hell forever those who hurt you. I pray God will make your lives exactly like your born-again hearts, with Jesus honored in every act, and His honoring you in all your dreams, as is the desire of His heart.

Don't let your willingness to believe God be taken for gullibility. I would never set any kind of dates for Christ's return to the earth, and don't you listen to anyone who does. The church will be caught away first, then anti-Christ will take over all religion. I told you before about anti-Christ, and now you know that your church itself, by its very presence, keeps him from taking over. After we all, living and dead, are caught away in the air to be with Jesus, the anti-Christ will appear for all to see, and then Jesus will return to earth in flaming judgment.

The anti-Christ will have all kinds of miracle-power and do many amazing things—just what hypocrites want—and God will harden their hearts and let them go to Hell.

I am so thankful that you will be in the Rapture because the Holy Spirit found your hearts and you believed the truth we preached. So don't listen to fanatics—just stick with the simple truth.

I need your prayers, for my work and for my safety. Of course, that is what we all need—and to keep our minds on love and steadfastness.

Have absolutely nothing to do with those second-coming fanatics who quit their jobs and expect Jesus immediately. That is contrary to all I preach and do: I, who, as a missionary planting churches, certainly am not required to work at night as a tentmaker. Just let idle busybodies starve to death, and go on working, working, working 'till Jesus comes.

I didn't say these fanatics are not Christians just shun them to shame them.

God give you peace in believing, always,

Paul

(I sign my epistles—that anonymous message which bothered you was a fraud.)

1 Timothy

Dear Timothy,

I write as an apostle to a pastor and as a father to a son.

Though we started together on this fourth missionary journey (I made three before my imprisonment at Rome) I must again ask you to remain as pastor there at Ephesus; that city is still a hot-bed of foolish religious babble.

So much talk is *so* worthless. Christianity produces a deep well of pure love in the soul of the believer. Arguments about religious rules are stagnant waters of ignorance. The rules God gave in the Old Testament were designed to control the raging appetites of depravity. Now, the simple gospel of Christ cleanses the most degenerate man in an instant.

Praise God, it worked on me! My religious fanaticism had made me an actual murderer— and nothing is worse than that! All those 'rules' failed, but the gospel worked. The whole story of humanity is pictured in my life and experiences and, thank God, illustrates the grand possibility of salvation available to all.

So, declare absolute war on all slaveries of the soul. Give no quarter to the men who reject the future that is now here.

The basics of living for the born-again are very simple:

Pray for political tranquility and use it to spread the Gospel, for our only task is to lift men to God through Jesus Christ—the only Saviour of men.

So pray, pray, pray. Let men and women cloth themselves in prayer for the evangelizing of the world. (God wants women to participate in all but not to lead the congregation or the home.)

The man who pastors a church must truly *want to*. He must strongly believe in the monogamous home. As he can't be a drunkard, so he can't be contentious and materialistic. His credentials must include leadership at home, experience in Christian work, and a reputation for decency and integrity in the community.

Those who hold official positions under the pastor must meet the same requirements.

These simple, self-evident standards are a far-cry from the elaborate rules and regulations of the false prophets and are designed to protect the congregation which is God's outpost in this world and the guardian of the majestic Christian

Creed—a creed which will always be distorted by people who wish to have other people subservient to them. They reject the spiritual progress represented by Christianity. Play these same notes over and over; like physical exercise, doing so will make you strong—strong enough to suffer for Christ.

Don't be intimidated by older men who don't see as clearly as you. Just do your best every hour of every day and you will be vindicated. Just show common respect to age and the weaker sex.

A widow who has relatives is not really a widow in that she has a family to support her; she should not be sustained by both family and church. A real widow is the responsibility of the congregation, but then only if she is sixty and has lived a life of humble service. Let a younger widow find herself a new husband.

A pastor must be paid a reasonable salary and no one should pay attention to accusations against him unless there are several eyewitnesses. And the entire congregational life must be conducted in democracy.

A man enters the ministry when a pastor ordains him. No one should be ordained who has not proven himself; without examination a drunkard might be ordained. (Of course there is a big difference between using wine as a health aid and being a drunkard.) In any event, careful examination of ministerial candidates will prevent many embarrassments.

173

Since the Christian life has nothing to do with material possessions, being an indentured slave is of no consequence—other than being an opportunity to imitate Jesus. A far worse condition is enslavement to the lust for material wealth.

It is our job as preachers to seek spiritual wealth and to share it. Think always of Jesus who stood a pauper before the wealth and power of the world, but stood as the King of Truth—yea, very God! Warn Christian men of the dangers in dreaming of wealth.

Forget about those ignorant attacks on the validity of Christianity.

God will help you,

Paul

2 Timothy

Dear Timothy,

I will live forever with Jesus Christ who saved me and made me His representative. As I face death here at Rome, I can say that I have never deviated in my life-long dedication to truth. My prayer is that you will not be discouraged by my execution. Indeed, identify with me, a condemned man (so was Jesus). Neither of us deserves to be a preacher—but we are both part of God's eternal plan unfolded in Jesus Christ, the Giver of eternal life. Yes, I am God's man and that is why I am condemned to die. My head is all I can possibly lose. You, by yourself, can insure that my message will live on. (You, along with Onesiphorus and his family, seem to be my only stalwarts left in Asia Minor.)

Now you must bear the responsibility of training preachers, and take my place as the SOLD-OUT SOLDIER OF THE CROSS. Remember the resurrection of Christ and how fanatics hate it and you will know exactly why I am reputed to be a criminal. But I am willing to suffer the death facing me for love of these very enemies.

I die for the same reason Christ died and I will triumph with Him forever, whether or not friend or foe believes it to be true. Be sure your student-preachers know these things.

As you teach God's message, never turn or twist—just go straight down the line. Ignore those who complicate God's Word, deny the future resurrection of the body and tolerate indecency. They are trash cans and you are a golden goblet—don't mix company. Let your gentle pleadings stand forever in contrast with their abrasive arguments.

The well of human depravity will never run dry and from its curb shall come an endless procession of religious reprobates. The Judgment will display the difference between them and myself. True, I suffered everywhere in Asia Minor (Turkey), but it was all for well doing. By no means will I be the last to suffer, for power-hungry men will always try to out-do one another and those who preach freedom and purity will be objects of their venom. Just move straight ahead and stick with the infallible Bible; every single passage and word is part of your equipment.

My last dying word is this:

Declare the whole counsel of God! Never hedge, dodge, or trim. People who do not hear the Word of God regularly will grow fond of the devil's lies. So never go to sleep on the job.

My work is done and my death is decreed. I will triumph for time and eternity. I am alone except for Dr. Luke. Please leave now with Mark, pick up my things at Troas, and hasten to my side.

Although many 'friends' have forsaken me, my great enemy, Alexander of Ephesus, has been always present to press his criminal charges which resulted in this second imprisonment. But he failed in his attempt to have me fed to lions. I preached in his presence and shouted the victory.

I want to see you before I die.

The little Roman church sends their love too.

Paul

Titus

Dear Titus,

There is one God, one Saviour, one creed, one church, one holy way of life, and one eternal hope, and I am God's voice preaching all these things which all born-again people believe.

As I continue this fourth missionary tour it is necessary for you to remain on the island of Crete to further the congregations there. Each one needs to elect a pastor, a man of exemplary conduct, even temper, generosity, and spiritual comprehension. Those loud-mouthed cultists who enslave people's minds by (among other approaches) appealing to family loyalties are interested only in money, power and their own bellies. Because they are filled with filthy emotions, they make evil things of both our Hebrew heritage and our Christian faith.

How different is our doctrine: we simply urge every segment of the congregation to enthrone purity, moderation, and gentleness. For the Gospel of Salvation is the enemy of moral laxity in any strata of society; it lifts all hearts and eyes to Heaven and the holy face of our returning Saviour. Let none minimize your authority in pressing these basic matters.

Remind all to be good citizens and to deport themselves with dignity and grace. When Christians see a degenerate sinner they should simply say "There I go, but for the Grace of God, the new birth, the indwelling power of the Holy Spirit and the blood of the Lord Jesus Christ."

Any so-called 'Bible teaching' which does not produce humility and purity is worthless and anyone addicted to it must be removed from the church roll if he refuses your repeated corrections.

Soon I will send a replacement for you and you can join me at my winter location in southern Greece. Help those other fellows who are planning their own missionary tour and encourage the home folk to know the joy of daily accomplishments.

Everyone here in northern Greece exchanges love to our loving brethren.

Grace,
Paul

Philemon

Dear Philemon (and dear friends),

When, as often, I pray for you, I also thank God for you. You are truly an example of a generous Christian man.

Now I appeal to your generosity, not for myself, (remember, I, in my sixties, am a prisoner here in Rome), but for your, now converted, runaway slave, Onesimus. He has been saved here in the services conducted in my room, and I truly love him as a son. I need and want him here, but in this situation there is an opportunity to display the Christian cure for the institution of slavery.

The evils of slavery must be destroyed through the new-birth: all born-again men are brothers. A converted slave is as noble as an apostle. To establish this brotherhood, I am willing to pay whatever price is required. But then, both you and Onesimus owe your exalted positions to me for service which I have already rendered in the preaching of the Gospel.

I am absolutely confident that born-again

men, instructed in the Gospel of Christ, will do more than is necessary to spread the brotherly love of Christianity—which is the best way to solve these awful human-relations problems.

You have prayed for my release from house-arrest. Prepare a guest-room for me; I am coming.

Many co-workers join me in this letter.

May God strengthen you,

,   Paul

Hebrews

Jesus Christ is God's Salvation. He is the Son of God, higher than all angels. In fact, He is to be recognized as very God. Moreover, this fact of His deity is essential to Christian faith. And He who rules eternity forsook His glory, not to be an angel—but a man, in order to save men.

Jesus is building a new nation, and it is a spiritual race. It has a 'land' of peace and rest entered only through decisive faith, and missed by those who only consider, but do not take, the step of total belief in Christ.

It is possible for Jews now, as in their past national history, to hear and know a lot—yet still miss the blessing of salvation.

Jews should accept the peace and rest Jesus offers, for it was clearly alluded to by David, whose words could not possibly refer to political peace

Jesus has peace and rest for today's Jews. They can have this true real High Priest who will meet their deepest spiritual needs. He has been provided for them by God the Father to be their timeless Benefactor, in so many wonderful ways.

But each Jew must make a clear decision, once and for all.

There are many born-again Jews, and they have certainly made that final decision. God the Father swears to them as He did to Abraham, and they know the peace that Jesus gives.

Jesus is the Heavenly priest of all nations. He is like that great mystery priest, Melchizidek, who stepped from nowhere to be honored of the greatest of all Hebrews, long before any national priesthood existed.

Now the national priesthood is passing away just at the time Jesus has become the eternal Priest—and His service for us shall never end. The Levitical system was quite insufficient, but Jesus is all sufficient. He will never die, never change; He is eternally perfect in all His attributes.

Yes, Jesus has been our spiritual High Priest since He arose and ascended to Heaven. The Old system cried out for change. Spiritual reality and freedom were demanded, and atonement had to be eternal.

The Jewish worship was always simply a physical representation of spiritual reality, and the fact was, men were actually shut out from God. Then Christ came, working in the realm of spiritual reality, and died the atoning death (the

Levitical system was also dedicated by blood) necessary to open up Heaven.

And Heaven is ours eternally because of Christ's once for all atonement.

The Jewish system was temporary and repetitive, and never God's ultimate desire. Christianity is God's eternal, timeless design. The Levitical system never actually accomplished anything, it simply foreshadowed the reality of Christ, and the 'born-again' experience. Ceremonial worship is now useless. The true Holy sanctuary is the person of Christ, our Spirit-filled bodies, and the congregation of believers. Rejection of Christ is without remedy, as equity and justice demand.

Many Jews have accepted much of Christ's teachings but they must not stop short of a full break with the past through decisive faith.

Invisible faith has always been more important than ceremony or racial identity, as a roll-call of Jewish history illustrates:

Abel worshipped by faith.

Enoch walked by faith.

Noah worked by faith.

Abraham traveled by faith.

Sarah conceived by faith.

Abraham risked all by faith.

185

Isaac promised by faith.

Jacob hoped by faith.

Joseph planned by faith.

Moses survived by faith.

Joshua conquered by faith.

Rahab was saved by faith.

Judges and prophets shaped the world through faith.

Christianity is the fulfillment of all their dreams.

The Christian church continues their heroic tradition by following Jesus, enduring hardships, responding correctly to God's discipline, and realizing the responsibility of being an example.

The church needs good men, and careful men, for it is now much more than Israel ever was: it is the true Temple of God for all men. It has God's message from Heaven.

Therefore, love. Love brothers, strangers, prisoners, sufferers; love all with deep empathy.

Guard your marriage relationship.

Beware of the temptations of money.

Respect your pastor, for he lives only for Christ.

Christianity will never change. It will always be persecuted by ritual-minded religionists. And believers will share Christ's rejection.

(Paul)

James

To the synagogues of 'THE WAY' all over the world:

Don't worry when you are persecuted for believing on Jesus Christ. You will grow and God will, with cosmic dependability, give you wisdom to meet every emergency. Just make up your mind to stand for Christ, no matter what.

The poor and the rich worship together in our synagogues; both must regard themselves as royalty and yet poverty-stricken. It is the man who wins in the hour of moral crisis who is rich. And every man must win this battle within himself. From Heaven alone comes the new nature imparted at the moment of the new birth, and this is the basis of all we say.

So let all be slow to criticize others. Let each clean up his own life. Remember the teachings of Jesus and give full-time to obeying them. A wagging tongue is tied to a twisted heart, but the born-again soul breathes love and compassion on the helpless, and longs for purity.

Remember, our synagogues are Christian assemblies and Christ is the Friend of the poor and lowly. To honor the rich is to repudiate Jesus who honors only *faith*.

Seek and honor the poor. All oppression comes from rich people, so to honor them for being rich is prohibited by God's Book. To so honor the rich breaks every Commandment.

Likewise, to turn from the needs of the poor is to repudiate Christianity and render invalid every pretense to Christian faith. From Abraham on, faith has always proven itself, and now, identification with the destitute is necessary to display Christian faith.

Before a man decides to teach others how to live, let him learn to control his own tongue. The steering gear is broken when the tongue is loose. The tongue has thermonuclear power; it can be dedicated to good or evil—but not both!

Your teachers must display purity and quiet thoughtfulness; a leader at war with a brother lies when he claims to teach truth. It is impossible! God's peacemakers exhibit the peace of God in their lives.

A frustrated Christian is a dangerous force. He will assassinate your character because he is filled with emotional confusion. His old nature dominates him, and, of course, it is made of nothing but psychological greed.

But no one *has to* be selfish. Admit your filthy tendencies and God will deliver you from the burning need to out do people. However, you must take the first step in this; it must be a profound facing of facts. And you will have to stop playing God—examining peoples hearts and passing opinions. You will have to stop your idle bragging—you who are no more than a wisp of smoke dissipating on the evening horizon. Only the present moment is yours; tomorrow may not come, you may not see the setting of the sun. So, to fail any priceless moment is a gross sin of arrogant pride.

And tomorrow, if it does come, will see the crashing of many a fortune. Your hordes of precious metals will be as much comfort as fire and acid. And such is fitting for you who gathered your riches from the sweat of the poor.

And you who suffer under the greedy rage of the rich must not partake of their sins; you must trust God to right the wrongs. And certainly don't envy your poor brother. Go back and read the Book of Job. Never, never let your sorrows make you bitter and cynical.

Let this be your philosophy: "I will pray when in trouble and sing when delivered. I will ask my fellow church members to touch God and me when I am sick. I will not hide my mistakes from the friends whose prayers I trust. I will stake my life

*on prayer! And I will not let my brother
fall away into discouragement, cynicism
and defeat."*

God's slave,

James

1Peter

Greetings to God's new 'people' scattered around the world, saved by the blood:

Our new family relationship includes an inheritance when we 'come of age,' so, all of our 'childhood lessons' are learned with joy, for we know what lies ahead.

The Hebrew prophets who wrote the Old Testament wondered how and when the great promises would begin to come true. God let them know they were to be for a time then future—now. So, think clearly about your great opportunity—and live the clean life it commands. Remember that God treats all His children alike, and that you were 'adopted' through the new birth at infinite cost. You accepted Christ because you wanted the life of holiness, sincerity, and philanthropy; He gave you just such hearts when you believed the Gospel, for the Gospel is God's reproductive seed creating an eternal family of pure and loving children.

So, despise ordinary, impure attitudes toward

your new family members. Just cry out for the 'milk' that produces healthy spiritual adults—pure, sincere, and honest thinking. You know how it tastes.

You came to Christ to build upon Him a new, clean life, and He is building you into a great Temple, with pure priests and ordinances.

This House shall never fall. Israel rejected the all-important Cornerstone, and her Temple fell—as any must. Now, all the promises of the prophets are coming true in the church of born-again pagans. (You must fight the 'enemies' in your own souls, as Israel had to fight her way to Canaan.)

Christianity recognizes the necessity of governments, and in no wise claims that Christians should be exempt. Our position is clear: respect every human being, respect the government, love the church, fear God.

You slaves who are under the government of owners must not rebel; this is your divine opportunity. Jesus was in a similar situation—He was so mistreated, He suffered so much—yet He quietly left His case in God's hands. And in so doing He became your Saviour, when He walked up to the Altar of Sacrifice and laid Himself down on the wood to pay for your sins and provide your new births to lives of purity. Jesus took the 'runaway-slave-beating' we 'runaway slaves' deserve, so now any one (for all are runaways from God) can come home to

God his Creator without fear of punishment.

Similar to the slave issue, Christian wives must honor their unsaved husbands. A Christian woman's greatest beauty is her reserved and quiet manner—especially in relation to her husband.

Christian husbands must submit too, (like the slaves) to their wives' feminine nature and weaknesses; God treats you both as His children.

Then, all Christians must submit (like the slaves) to all other Christians.

Now, who in the world will punish you for living this life of Christian love, tranquility, and submission. If someone does, you can know with a clear conscience that you are suffering just like your Lord Jesus, when He became your substitute sacrifice.

Evil men cannot touch the soul. As it is in your civilization, so degenerates persecuted Noah in his—because he wanted to be saved from its impurity, and from God's wrath upon it. And, in the ark, he was lifted above the ungodly by the flood which killed them. So the waters of baptism picture the same present situation—you desire the pure life, and have chosen Jesus as Saviour from the impure life and its judgment. You are, by being included in Christ's substitutionary sufferings, saved from the wrath of this ungodly world, and from God's wrath upon its impurity. Not by superstitious washing of the body, but because God, in your new births, actually cleaned up your lives. this is what baptism displays—Noah's ark lifted the eight saved people above the filthy world, and Jesus' resurrection takes us right into Heaven, while delivering us from both the ungodly civilization we are in, and its judgment.

So, think of yourselves as having already died physically, and now permitted a second life just so you can live to honor God's purity. Your first life (which you now consider dead) was impure, and the old crowd who did not 'die' see you as the same old person. They must stand condemned before God one day (at their death), but the good news is that you are counted by God to have already died—in Jesus your substitute—and have been raised spiritually from that death to live a second, new life.

When you die physically—it won't be long—your wonderful opportunity to live clean and submissive lives in a dirty and selfish world will be over; so, fill yourselves with love to serve one another and to use your abilities to honor God.

In your daily troubles you are experiencing the same kind of persecutions Jesus received—and when He is rewarded, you will be also. Just be sure your testimony is crystal clear. The time of your reward—or embarrassment—is near, be sure you are not embarrassed by merely being saved, with no reward for scars. (How horrible what the lost shall receive! They shall suffer in body and in spirit—forever.)

Pastors, as loving shepherds and examples—not dictators—care for your churches. You'll receive eternal recognition.

Every church member must honor the pastor—in fact, honor one another in humility. And give your personal problems to Jesus, don't take them out on fellow believers. Satan is everyone's enemy.

Pain will be forgotten in the victories of Jesus.

Silas is delivering this letter. He, Mark, and I live in the heart of this world's wicked culture—BABYLON—Rome herself, and there is a congregation like yours here, too.

Give my kiss of love to one another.

Peace in Jesus be yours,

Peter,

Apostle and Pastor

2 Peter

Dear Fellow Believers,

Let us get to know Jesus even better. To know Christ and His promises is to be ready for everything in life and death. This knowledge of the Saviour is the foundation on which to build your personal temple of praise and productivity. But to stop short is to raise questions about the validity of one's profession of faith. If you have a desire to know Christ fully, that is evidence of your new birth and all it represents.

Until I die *(Jesus said I would be killed before His return)*, I want to constantly remind all Christians to go on with Christ, and I want everyone to read my encouragements after I am gone. When I talk about Jesus I am speaking from personal eyewitness experience; I even heard the Father's voice at the Transfiguration. And I have interpreted all I saw and heard in the light of the Old Testament Scriptures, every one of which was dictated by God Himself.

Nevertheless, men have never (and will never) stop corrupting God's truth. Their motive is always to enslave a following. God hates that, and as surely as He punished angels and men of the past, He will judge present-day enemies of correct biblical interpretation.

Let me give a 'Bill of Attainder': They lust for power; They are arrogant; They walk with foolish ignorance where angels fear to tread; They dishonestly want to worship as Christians, while despising the freedom promised by the gospel; they hypocritically talk of freedom *(they themselves are slaves to their lust for power)*. A limited *infatuation* with Christ made them look good for awhile, but they are no more than dogs who sniff good food and then cough up their old meal and re-eat it. If a pig is not born again into a sheep, it will always love mud.

I insist you all pay close and constant attention to the Old Testament and how Christ's Apostles interpreted it. Let no new interpreter deny the ultimate triumph of Christ in His second coming. Just as the first civilized order was suddenly, without current events so indicating, destroyed by the Great Flood, so the last civilized order shall be destroyed by the Great Fire. There is no hurry, for God's love is at work. But the day will come when the atoms of all atmospheric gases will burn with unspeakable fury—as well as Earth itself.

We do not look for signs and are not moved by the absence of them. We just look for that new day and the hope it represents. I am in perfect agreement with Paul in this and all matters and condemn those who misuse his letters in the same way they abuse the Old Testament.

Let us learn more and more about Jesus.

Praise Him forever,

Peter

1 John

Eternity has spoken and I have heard, more than that—TOUCHED AND SEEN. Yes, I walked with God Himself through Galilee and Judea, so many years ago. We still walk together, and you, my children, can walk with Him too.

How do we do that, now that He is in Heaven? We live by His teachings of love and trust His atoning death to forgive our hateful sins; love cannot be divorced from truth, and the truth is that we all fail sometimes in the obedience of love.

No, no one has to sin, but Jesus Christ is the Saviour for the whole world because no one in the world has reached sinless perfection. But we who have been born again know that we love His law of love; we say it and we mean it because we think of it constantly.

Love is our law, love is our sunshine—daybreak from our night of hate. Love that difficult person near you and you love God; scorn him and you confess yourself to be an imposter. Let all the born-again, young and old, be as tiny little children—eager and willing to love.

But please, please don't love 'things,' for that is greed and far removed from God. He cares not what you have—He will walk with you forever and ever. People who preach the love of God in Christ have no problem in declaring the deity of Jesus. No one is a Christian who denies that Jesus is the true God.

There is God the Father, Creator of all things, God the Son who walked among us, and God the Holy Spirit who touches our consciences and makes it easy to know these truths and to recognize false teachings.

Because He loves us, we are born-again and in His family of love. We will grow up to be exactly like Him in love when we see the shining face of Jesus at His second coming. Our hearts burn within us now to be like Him in holiness, truth and love.

Love and sin cannot reign in the same heart; no Christian ever preached anything to the contrary. There are *two* families of men: the unsaved—full of hate and impurity, and the born-again—full of purity and love.

LOVE, LOVE, LOVE—that is the message now and forever. Men hate even their natural brothers, but Christians have a supernatural love which makes it possible to love born-again nobodies to the point that we will give all we have to meet their needs. The only way to love is to give to our brother until it hurts.

Oh, to love like this is infinite peace. God will surely give anything requested to the person who gives his all to his brother in need.

The Jesus who taught us this love is God. It should be easy and simple to reject all teachers who deny the deity of our Christ. Such prophets are of Satan and thoroughgoing materialists—they lust for 'things' and power over men. We whose only law is love will be honored by all who know the love of God; of the others, beware.

Remember, there are *birth-marks* on the born-again. The *first one* is this miracle-love they have for one another—it can only come from understanding that Jesus died as our substitute to save their souls. The *second* is the indwelling presence of the Holy Spirit—there is something new speaking in our hearts. The *third birth-mark* is the joy with which we confess that Jesus Christ our Saviour is very God. The *fourth* is the absence of fear in our emotions. We fear to lose nothing, we will not lose God as our Father and we cannot lose possessions for we are longing to give them away to our brother in need.

Now you can see how accepting Christ as Saviour is the act that brings the new birth. Love floods the soul of the born-again—a love for men and a rejection of materialism. All of this is self-evidently miraculous; it is possible for any person to have the absolute assurance of eternal salvation.

That is exactly why I have written this letter; I want you to rejoice in this assurance that God has saved your souls and will answer all your prayers. (Pray effectively for your brother, even when he sins.)

There are two families of man; materialistic, hateful men; and non-materialistic, loving men. Accept Jesus Christ as Saviour-God and you are born-again into His family of love.

Remember love and purity,

John

2 John

Dear Christians, old and new,

I love you. Everyone who loves truth loves the church. God multiply your blessings.

I'm so glad you are making converts and that they are 'sticking.' They are living the Gospel of Love. It is the Gospel of Christ—the only good news in this world. Anyone who gives aid and comfort to religious teachers who deny the historical facts of the Incarnation and the simple love gospel is quilty of betrayal.

I will visit your congregation soon.

John

3 John

Dear Gaius,

Your wonderful personal testimony is spreading far and wide. I wish your body were as strong as your soul.

The preaching team I sent out (Jewish Christians) was overwhelmed by the generosity you show to everyone. How different from one of your pastors—a power-hungry mad-man. As a faithful church member you will just have to listen to everything but do only that which is right.

There is another man who would make a fine pastor. But I will come and speak to you personally about that.

Say "Hello" to my friends.

John

Jude

To all Christians:

Because you have heard and believed the Gospel of God's love, you are eternally safe in Jesus Christ.

Your salvation (and mine) is wonderful—so wonderful that we must oppose with all our might the people who sneak into our circles and try to spread their denial of the Christian creed. You can be sure their motives are filthy. Their arrogance is unbounded. They are mastered by animal-like instincts.

To the flames with them! They hate mankind, they prostitute religion, they rebel against the Christian revelation.

These 'shepherds' shear, slaughter, skin and eat the sheep. Their souls are empty, their roots are rotten, their hearts are full of filth. They lead men only into vacant nothingness.

God will stop their mouths—mouths which prey upon the ignorance and vanity of men.

Remember, those who make ceremony,

ritual, regimen, diet, race or any external, physical thing essential—or important—in religion are not themselves inhabited by the Spirit of God.

But Christians have a spiritual creed and are temples of God himself. Love, mercy, eternal hope in Jesus Christ—this is Christianity. Yes, mercy for the weak and love to rescue those who are being engulfed in the burning passions of unspeakable immorality.

Praise God for the Creed is true, the Spirit is real, salvation is sure; the only true God is our Saviour through His incarnation in Jesus Christ.

Amen,

Jude

Revelation

Prologue

The consumation of history was unveiled by the Lord Jesus Christ, through a Heavenly messenger, who showed it to John the Apostle.

This is a faithful recording of the Divine communication and is to be read, with expectations of spiritual profit, in the official Sunday services of Christian congregations everywhere.

❧❧❧❧❧❧❧❧❧❧❧❧❧❧❧

My own dear congregations, representing the beauties of Heaven and Earth,

The Lord Jesus greets you too! He has told us the truth about everything. He arose from the dead—and will raise us up; He has more power and authority than all governments. Let us praise and surrender all to Him, for His love and cleansing blood have made every one of us personal representatives of the true and living God.

I can see Him now, returning with myriads of angels, forcing everyone—even His murderers and His many pagan enemies—to see Him. He is very God, in whose infinite purpose all history moves toward eternal fulfillment.

JESUS IS THE HIGH PRIEST OF THE CHURCHES

Though in exile on this lonely island, I was, as usual, having special worship on a certain Sunday when a blaring voice shook my meditations.

Start recording this vision, and send your account to your congregations in Turkey.

—And there was Jesus, as Eternal High Priest of all the churches. The pastors belong to Him and the Bible is His Book. He has unlocked the doors of death—from inside! He told me to be calmed. And to write all.

Pastor at Ephesus: tell your congregations that although they have rejected vile paganism and tyrannical ritualistic religion, it is not enough—they must get back to evangelizing the lost. Although opposing evil is essential, it is those who do both who will enjoy a sweet peace and joy known only by soul-winners who walk close to Me.

Pastor At Smyrna: guard your flock from religious apostates. Times of great testing lie ahead—death on every hand. Remember, death's sting is dead.

Pastor of Pergamos: Your creed is pure, but those in your church who think they can eat at My table and at the table of pagan idols must repent. Yearn for the pure spiritual food, the pure heart, the pure reputation.

Pastor of Thyatira: your church has so many good qualities, but it is a false generosity to allow a woman who is no more than a prostitute to have unhindered opportunity to ruin the lives of Christian people. She is promoting vile filth under the guise of 'life's deeper insights.' This is your one, big problem. Don't sacrifice My purpose for you—I want you, through the Gospel, to shake and shape the world, to give it hope every single day!

Pastor at Sardis: your church is all but a dead shell. You are asleep on the job. You are mistreating the few whose hearts still long for the old spiritual paths. I will walk with them now and forever.

Pastor at Philadelphia: your small church is doing magnificent things—Heaven is with you. Your bitter religious adversaries will someday change their tunes. The world's calamities can't touch you; I will deliver you! Your positions in the eternal Temple of Truth are fixed forever. All that is God's is yours.

Pastor of Laodicea: your congregation is a jumble of contradictions. Money can buy nothing eternal. Bring pure hearts and

215

humble spirits to My storehouse. I cannot permit your strange half-heartedness. I have been excluded from your rich materialistic programs, but I still am searching out sincere hearts for fellowship. They alone can reign with me.

JESUS IS THE ONLY MEDIATOR BETWEEN GOD AND MAN

Then I saw into Heaven. And then that trumpet voice commanding me to COME. There I was at God's throne. The colorful radiance was dazzling. I saw the Church of all the ages, brought there by all the infinite powers of God's Holy Spirit—no more cleansings necessary. The Cherubim which guard the purity of Heaven sing, with the Church there, of holiness forever, and the redeemed join in the praise. The dilemma of redemption—a man must be creation's redeemer—has been solved by Jesus, the slain Lamb. So, Heaven sings the Song of Salvation.

The Lamb of God is involved in the history of mankind. Empires are built and wars ensue, producing famine and epidemic death: in all this people are born again and suffer for the Faith. But all accounts will be settled at the Second Coming of Christ, at which there will be glorification for born-again Jews, and born-again Gentiles. Heaven will salute the triumph of the Lamb of God.

JESUS IS THE JUDGE OF EVIL MEN

When the trumpets of Judgment sound, the

earth will be devastated, the oceans will be filled with blood, rivers will flow with death, and clouds will roll with doom. Demon hordes will torture humanity who have refused God's salvation. Armies will kill multitudes—a third of all peoples. The final holocaust will be too horrible to consider. But before then, redemption will reach multitudes, God will be worshipped in Spirit as His Truth will be boldly preached. The Lord's preachers will finish their mission and triumph over their enemies. Yes, God's justice will be celebrated.

JESUS IS THE ETERNAL VICTOR

The Saviour was promised before the world began, but Lucifer (Satan) rebelled against the plan. In time, the Deliverer was born, and Satan, expelled from Heaven for his rebellion, lied to mankind. However, the living God promised salvation, and, though His people are persecuted by Satan, they will triumph. Satan's men will have power to amaze the world so that Satan's false prophet can deceive and regiment the race, but Jesus will triumph, with born-again Jews and born-again Gentiles. Satan's religious and political tyranny will be punished forever. King Jesus will gather His 'wheat' and the 'tares' will be eternally burned.

JESUS IS THE JUDGE OF ALL MEN

The redeemed will sing as judgment is

prepared: cancerous disease, oceans of death, rivers of death, intense heat, darkness and pain, and marching armies, for it will mark the end of the apparent ascendency of Satan.

JESUS IS THE JUDGE OF FALSE SALVATION SYSTEMS

So often, 'religious' evil cohorts with political crimes and lives in arrogance. They support each other in the Secular City. But all political tyranny shall be destroyed—after that oppressive system smashes the religious tyranny. Today, many profit from tyrannies (of which Christians can have no part)—politicians, businessmen, merchants. Christians will have great profit in evil's destruction.

JESUS IS THE FINAL JUDGE OF THE DESTINIES OF MEN

False religionists are to be punished—forever! But believers will be with Christ forever. Political empires will be destroyed at the Second Coming of Christ and Satan's domain will be consigned to the Lake of Fire. Not a single born-again believer will taste the fires of eternal death. It is Satan who will be imprisoned in Hell forever, along with all those who did not want the born-again life of simplicity and purity in Christ.

The eternal condition of the born-again will be a glorious new reality: there shall be no more tears, and no more poverty; they shall live in the

New City of brilliance, majesty, Godliness, and eternal day. They will enjoy fellowship with God forever, through Jesus Christ their Lord. Yes, this is the certainty of Christianity and the fulfillment of all spiritual history. There is futility in all other hopes. Christ is the only hope, and aside from Him there is only despair. He is the Promise we received yesterday, He is the hope we have for tomorrow, and He is the Invitation that is pressed today.

Now, I, John, warn all men that the truth of Jesus Christ—His salvation and eternal victory—must not be altered, and it must not be minimized—not so much as a tiny word.

Jesus shall reign.

FREE

- Parchment-like -
- Suitable for framing -

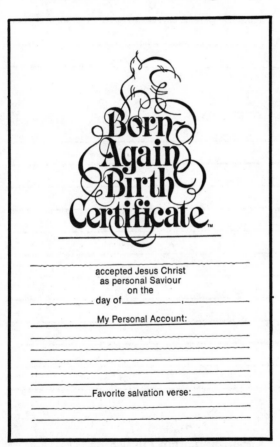

Born~Again Birth Certificate

_____ accepted Jesus Christ
as personal Saviour
on the
_____ day of _____, _____

My Personal Account:

_____
_____
_____
_____

_____ Favorite salvation verse: _____
_____
_____

Born-Again Birth Certificate

Please send my FREE Born-Again Birth Certificate.

Name _____

Address _____

_____ Zip _____

Readers Comments:

_____
_____
_____
_____
_____
_____
_____
_____
_____
_____

mail to
Paul Benjamin Publishers
P.O. Box 1207
Stone Mountain, Georgia 30086

OTHER EDITIONS AVAILABLE

Enjoy The *Distilled* Bible/New Testament
as read by Author on cassettes.
24.95   _____

Giant Print 9¾ x 7¼ limpback
9.95   _____

Deluxe Gift Edition, cloth bound
12.95 9¾ x 7¼   _____

(prices include postage, handling
and applicable tax.)

Total Enclosed   _____

☐ Collectors Editiion of entire *Distilled* Bible O.T.
and N.T. for delivery spring 1981. (You will be
billed 30 days before shipping.) 59.95

☐ Please provide information on bulk discounts
for fund raising etc.

☐ Please send a FREE Born-Again Birth Certificate.

Name _____

Address _____

_____ Zip _____

Total Amount Enclosed _____

Readers Comments:

_____

_____

_____

_____

_____

_____

_____

_____

_____

_____

_____

_____

mail to:
Paul Benjamin Publishers
P.O. Box 1207
Stone Mountain, Georgia 30086